W9-CNY-017

Wholesale and Retail Trade in Tanganyika

A STUDY OF DISTRIBUTION IN EAST AFRICA

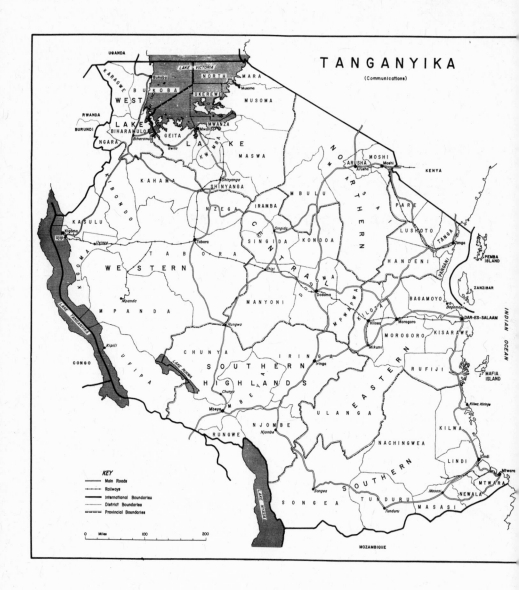

PRAEGER SPECIAL STUDIES IN
INTERNATIONAL ECONOMICS AND DEVELOPMENT

Wholesale and Retail Trade in Tanganyika

A STUDY OF DISTRIBUTION IN EAST AFRICA

H. C. G. HAWKINS

Prepared by

THE ECONOMIST INTELLIGENCE UNIT *for*
FREDERICK A. PRAEGER, *Publishers*
New York • Washington • London

The purpose of the Praeger Special Studies is to make specialized research monographs in international economics and politics available to the academic, business, and government communities. For further information, write to the Special Projects Division, Frederick A. Praeger, Publishers, 111 Fourth Avenue, New York, N.Y. 10003.

FREDERICK A. PRAEGER, *Publishers*
111 Fourth Avenue, New York 3, N.Y., U.S.A.
77-79 Charlotte Street, London W.1, England

Published in the United States of America in 1965
by Frederick A. Praeger, Inc., Publishers

Library of Congress Catalog Card Number: 65-12927

Printed in the United States of America

FOREWORD

The investigation on which this study is based was carried out by the author as a member of the staff of the Economist Intelligence Unit Limited at the request of the Tanganyika Ministry of Commerce and Industry during the five months from April to August 1962. The original report was prepared during the remaining months of 1962.

Though the research was carried out during 1962, the changes which have taken place in the last few years in the structure and operations of the distribution system in Tanganyika have not been very extensive, and the information contained in this study is still both relevant and of practical value to anyone interested in the problems of distribution in Tanganyika.

The survey was conducted by means of extensive interviewing of a representative selection of importers, wholesalers and retailers throughout the country. Two hundred and twenty full-scale interviews were carried out, together with a great many briefer interviews with the smaller retailers in both urban and rural areas. Forty-five of the fifty-five districts of Tanganyika were visited, and a distance of 8, 500 miles was covered by road.

The author wishes to thank the members of both the Dar es Salaam Chamber of Commerce and of the Dar es Salaam Merchants Chamber for their generous co-operation and assistance during the course of the investigation.

ACKNOWLEDGEMENT

Grateful acknowledgement is made to the Ministry of Commerce and Industry for its kind permission to publish the original report in its present form.

CONTENTS

Wholesale and Retail Trade in Tanganyika

A STUDY OF DISTRIBUTION IN EAST AFRICA

CHAPTER 1   CHARACTERISTICS OF THE TANGANYIKA ECONOMY

THE COUNTRY AND THE PEOPLE

Tanganyika lies just south of the equator on the east coast of Africa. It is the largest of the three former British East African territories, with an area of 362,000 square miles, almost as large as Venezuela and nearly 30 per cent larger than Texas, and with a population in 1961 of 9,400,000, of whom 108,000 were of Indian or Pakistani origin, 25,000 of Arab and 22,000 of European origin.

The boundaries of Tanganyika run through Lake Tanganyika to the west, Lake Victoria to the north and Lake Nyasa to the south; to the east there is a 500-mile coastline on the Indian Ocean. The flat coastal plain varies between ten and forty miles in width. Here the climate is tropical, hot and humid with a yearly average temperature of 76° F. and an average rainfall of 40 inches. Behind the coastal plain rises the great central plateau, averaging 3,000 feet above sea level and covering the greater part of the country. The climate of the plateau is hot and dry with a yearly average temperature of over 70° F. and rainfall of 10 to 40 inches. The nights are cool and the temperature shows great daily and seasonal variations. In the north of the country, Kilimanjaro, Africa's highest mountain rises to 19,340 feet. In the south the Southern Highlands form a large area rising about 5,000 feet. Here the climate is semi-temperate with warm days and cool nights and an average rainfall of 50 inches.

The predominant types of vegetation are bushland and wooded grassland; much of the centre of the territory is arid bush country. Approximately 60 per cent of the total land area is infested with tsetse fly which prevents its use for cattle-raising. There are comparatively small areas of tropical rain forest in the highland regions. The agricultural potential of Tanganyika is limited over large areas by soils of inherently low nutrient status. Extensive areas of really fertile land are confined to the volcanic soils of parts of the highlands in the Northern, Southern and Southern Highlands Regions, and to alluvial soils in the larger river valleys. Less than 30,000 square miles is under active cultivation.

The African population consists of 122 tribes, only one of which, the Sukuma on the southern shores of Lake Victoria, numbers as much as one million. Nearly all the tribes in Tanganyika are members of the East Bantu social group, using Swahili as a lingua franca. The Bantu are by tradition agriculturists or pastoralists, cultivating tribal land on a system of common tenure, and agriculture and livestock-raising remain the principal occupations.

THE HISTORICAL SETTING

The history of modern economic development in Tangan-yika is extremely short, having begun when the Union for Ger-man Colonization was founded in 1884. Before that date the principal contact of the inland parts of the territory with the non-African world was with Arab trading caravans and slave-raiders. Up to the end of the Second World War economic de-velopment was for a number of reasons somewhat sporadic.

From 1884 to 1918 the territory was a German colony known as German East Africa. In the 30 years prior to the outbreak of the First World War the Germans devoted much money and energy to the development of plantation agriculture, introducing sisal, coffee, tea, cotton, rubber and cinchona. Two railways were built, one from Tanga to Moshi, the other from Dar es Salaam to Kigoma. After the end of the war, a League of Nations mandate was given to the United Kingdom to administer the territory. In the period, 1925-29, a phase of rapid expansion took place, exports rising in value from $2.8 million in 1921 to $11.2 million in 1928. Efforts were made for the first time to induce African smallholders to pro-duce cash crops, mainly of cotton and coffee. This period was brought to an end by the depression and subsequently by political uncertainties as to the future of the territory.

In 1946 Tanganyika became a United Nations Trust Terri-tory under British administration, and in the post-war years the pace of economic development was vastly accelerated. The value of exports rose from $31.1 million to $140.3 million in 1961.

On December 9, 1961, Tanganyika became independent with Dr Julius Nyerere as Prime Minister. Subsequently Dr Nyerere became President of the Republic of Tanganyika which remains within the British Commonwealth.

Tanganyika's place in East Africa
    The economy of Tanganyika has close links with those of
Kenya and Uganda. As a result of the common British administration of the three countries, a customs union has long been
established and there is a common East African currency.
Although each country is autonomous in fixing its customs
tariff, there is in practice almost complete uniformity, and
no customs duties are levied on inter-territorial trade. The
East African Common Services Organisation administers, in
addition to the customs and excise, the income tax, railways
and harbours, civil aviation, posts and telegraphs, telephone
and radio communications and research.

THE STRUCTURE OF THE ECONOMY

GROSS DOMESTIC PRODUCT BY INDUSTRIAL ORIGIN 1960-62, AVERAGED.

Industrial Origin	Monetary Sector $ million	Subsistence Sector $ million	Total $ million	Percent of Total
Crop-husbandry, livestock, fishing	125.7	163.5	289.2	56.0
Forest products	3.1	4.2	7.3	1.4
Mining and quarrying	14.6	–	14.6	2.8
Processing and manufacturing	20.7	–	20.7	4.0
Public utilities	3.6	–	3.6	0.7
Construction	17.6	–	17.6	3.4
Transport and communications	24.4	–	24.4	4.7
Distribution	61.9	–	61.9	12.0
Rents and royalties	22.4	–	22.4	4.3
Public administration	35.3	–	35.3	6.8
Other services	19.3	–	19.3	3.7
Total	348.6	167.7	516.3	100.0

Source   Tanganyika Statistical Abstract

The Tanganyikan Gross Domestic Product averaged $516.3 million in the years 1960-62. About two-thirds of the total output is attributed to the monetary sector of the economy and the remainder to the product of subsistence farmers. The industrial origin of the G.D.P. is set out in the table above, from which the heavy dependence on agriculture clearly emerges, just under 60 per cent of the total being directly attributable to the agricultural sector. Manufacturing industry contributed only 4 per cent of the total and over half of this is made up by secondary agricultural processing and by food products and beverages. After agriculture, commerce, with 12 per cent of the total, was by far the largest contributor.

The economy of Tanganyika has developed primarily through the growth of exports of primary products, mainly agricultural and livestock products, to which in recent years have been added diamonds. The major export commodity is sisal, valued at $39.3 million in 1961, accounting for 29 per cent of total domestic exports. Cotton and coffee each made up a further 14 per cent and diamonds 12 per cent. On the export side Tanganyika has the good fortune to be relatively well-diversified; though sisal clearly remains dominant. Other major exports in order of importance are meat and meat preparations, cashew nuts, hides and skins, tea, gold and a variety of oilseeds.

PRINCIPAL DOMESTIC EXPORTS, 1961

	$ million	Per cent of total
Sisal	39.3	28.8
Cotton, raw	19.2	14.1
Coffee, not roasted	18.9	13.9
Diamonds	16.1	11.8
Meat and meat preparations	5.8	4.3
Cashew nuts	5.0	3.7
Hides and skins	4.9	3.6
Tea	3.7	2.7
Gold	3.5	2.6
All other items	19.8	14.5
Total	136.2	100.0

Source Annual Trade Report.

Estates account for all but a small fraction of Tanganyika's production of sisal, of which the territory is by far the most important world producer. The estates are concentrated mainly in the Tanga Region, along the Central Line between Dar es Salaam and Kilosa and in the area of Lindi and Mtwara in the Southern Region. Cotton in contrast is grown almost exclusively on African smallholdings, nearly 90 per cent coming from the area to the south and east of Lake Victoria.

Arabica coffee is produced mainly on the slopes of Kiliman-jaro and Mt. Meru. Robusta coffee is grown in the Bukoba and Karagwe districts west of Lake Victoria. The robusta crop is entirely produced on African smallholdings, though 50 per cent of the arabica is estate-grown. Cashew nuts are grown by smallholders almost entirely in the Southern and Eastern Regions. A great variety of other oil nuts and oilseeds, such as groundnuts, copra, sesame and castor seed, is grown in different parts of the country by smallholders. Tea, like sisal, is mainly an estate crop grown in the Southern Highlands and the Usambara Mountains in Tanga Region.

The herding of livestock, especially cattle, is widespread throughout the country, but while the number of animals is great, the contribution they make to the material product of the country is small. There is wasteful overstocking in many areas with consequent overgrazing and impoverishment of the soil. The main cattle-raising areas are in the Lake, Central and Northern Regions. Canning factories supplying both the home and export markets are located at Dar es Salaam and Arusha.

Diamonds are far and away the most important of the mine-rals currently being exploited in Tanganyika. Virtually the entire production comes from the Mwadui deposit of the Williamson Diamond Mines discovered in 1940. Scattered deposits of gold are also worked in the area east of Lake Victoria and in the Southern Highlands.

Manufacturing industry is at a very early stage of develop-ment in Tanganyika, and as we have already seen this sector contributes barely 4 per cent of the total Gross National Pro-duct. Less than 25,000 workers are employed in manufacturing. Most firms are small, family concerns and activities such as grain milling, cotton ginning, saw milling, woodwork and vehicle repairs make up a substantial part of this figure. In the past, Kenya, particularly the Nairobi area, has attracted most of the manufacturing industry in East Africa. The most important industries established in Tanganyika are brewing, wheat flour milling, meat packing, sugar refining, textiles, cigarettes,

shoes and tin cans. Most of these industries are located in the
Dar es Salaam area, though some are to be found at Arusha,
Moshi and Mwanza.

COMMUNICATIONS

   The railways provide the country with its main arterial com-
munications, except in the south and south-western areas.   The
Central Line more or less bisects the country, running from
Dar es Salaam on the Indian Ocean in the east to Kigoma on
Lake Tanganyika in the west, with a branch line running north
from Tabora to Mwanza on Lake Victoria.   A frequent lake
steamer service makes the circuit of Lake Victoria, connecting
Mwanza with Kisumu, the railhead in Kenya, as well as with
Jinja and Entebbe in Uganda.   A short branch line runs south
from Kilosa to Mikumi.   The Tanga Line runs from Tanga to
Moshi and Arusha, and Moshi is also linked by rail with
Mombasa.
   The main roads are laid out in a somewhat irregular grid
pattern with three running north and south and three running
east and west.   None can be classified as completely all-weather
for the whole of their length.   Nowhere, except in the neighbour-
hood of the main towns does the traffic exceed 500 vehicles per
24 hours.   There are 3, 860 miles of roads classified as all-
weather and 21, 460 miles of main and district roads, which are
not all-weather.   In 1961 there were 42, 256 motor vehicles
registered of which 17, 376 were passenger cars.

2

THE BACKGROUND
TO DISTRIBUTION
IN TANGANYIKA

FACTORS AFFECTING DISTRIBUTION

Sparse and scattered population

Tanganyika, with 362,000 square miles of territory, had an estimated population of only 9,400,000 in 1961. This represents an overall density of just over 27 persons per square mile. Distances are great. From the port of Dar es Salaam to the Lake Region, the largest single market in Tanganyika, it is over 750 miles by rail; from Dar es Salaam to the next largest market, the Moshi-Arusha area, is 400 miles by road, while from Moshi in the north to the Rungwe District at the northern end of Lake Nyasa in the south is 800 miles by road - sugar from Moshi is regularly carried over this route with a return load of rice from Rungwe.

The main centres of population, and therefore of purchasing power, are not grouped conveniently together as they are in Kenya and Uganda. In Kenya over 90 per cent of the population lives in less than 25 per cent of the total land area, and the Mombasa-Uganda railway runs right through the middle of this densely populated area. Likewise in Uganda, in any case a much smaller country, the population is heavily concentrated in a belt round Lake Victoria. In Tanganyika the areas of high density are scattered round the borders of the country at the greatest possible distances from each other. The largest concentrations of population are in the Lake Region; Bukoba; Moshi and Arusha; Tanga and Lushoto; along the Central Line from Dar es Salaam to Dodoma; the Southern Highlands, particularly in the Rungwe District; and in the Lindi, Mtwara, Newala and Masasi Districts of the Southern Region. A glance at the map will show that there is no single centre which is conveniently placed to serve all or even most of these areas.

Poor communications

Communications, though they have been improved considerably in the last few years, are not good. Until 1962 there was no all-weather road between the Lake, West Lake and Western Regions and the rest of Tanganyika. Thus, for at least three months of the year, during the rainy season, and often for longer, the only link

these Regions had with the rest of the country was a single
railway line. The whole of the Southern Region is still cut
off by land from the rest of Tanganyika for five or six months
in the year.

In certain areas a population of as many as 50,000 can be
cut off for weeks, sometimes months at a time, so that all
supplies have to be brought in by porters carrying head-loads.
In some parts of the Western and Southern Regions a small
retail shop may be more than 100 miles from the nearest
wholesaler. Clearly these circumstances add greatly to the
problems of distribution.

Size of the market

In addition to the immense distances, the scattered population and the poor communications, a further factor affecting
the distribution system in Tanganyika is the small size of the
market. The total Domestic Product in 1961 was $523.6
million. However, almost 40 per cent of this was contributed
by the subsistence sector of the economy. The total value of
marketed goods and services was estimated at $317.6 million
in 1961, which gives an annual cash income of $33.6 per head,
compared with G.D.P. per head in the United Kingdom of $1,246.

Subsistence production provides most needs

The fact that the subsistence sector of the economy forms
so large a part of the total has an important bearing on the
distribution system. In a highly developed economy practically all consumer requirements are obtained through the distribution system, i.e. by purchases for cash from various
types of retailers. Some vestiges of subsistence farming remain in such countries as England where many people grow
some of their fruit and vegetables in back gardens or on allot-
ments. However, the normal way of obtaining all requirements is to buy them from a shop.

In Tanganyika, on the other hand, most of the population produces most of its own day-to-day requirements. People buy for
cash from a shop only a comparatively small part of their requir
ments. The average family grows its own staple foodstuffs and
produces most of its own household utensils and furniture. The
only foodstuff which many families buy regularly is salt, though
often home-grown foodstuffs will be supplemented with purchases
of tea, sugar, rice, and maize meal, these last probably bought
when home-grown staple foods are scarce. Such items as clay
cooking pots, baskets, gourds, mortars and pounding poles, bas
kets, sleeping mats and stools, to mention only a few, are made
by members of the family. There has of course always been a
certain amount of specialisation in the production of these items,

and this is undoubtedly increasing. Cooking pots, mats, beds and pombe for instance are likely to be produced by specialists, but these items are not sold in shops, they are bartered or bought from individuals or in markets.

Many Africans have only minimal contacts with the mone - tary economy. The great majority are in an intermediate posi - tion, depending upon subsistence production for most of their staple wants, but selling some cash crops and buying some goods and services for money, so that in varying degrees they are partly in the subsistence economy and partly in the mone - tary economy. An increasing number are wholly in the mone - tary economy, that is earning wages or salaries. In 1961 there were just under 400, 000 Africans reported in paid employment. But a very large proportion of these also had a shamba on which members of their family were growing their own food. Besides those in employment, more and more Africans are growing cash crops, and earning sizable cash incomes in this way. Neverthe - less, production of cash crops is generally looked on as an acti - vity taking second place to production of food for the family. Even most African coffee growers regard coffee as subsidiary to their bananas, though among the Sukuma of the Lake Region the growing of cotton is gradually taking priority over all other forms of agriculture. The economy of Sukumuland is thus be - coming more and more a cash economy, and the people are be - coming increasingly dependent on the commercial distribution system.

The existence of the subsistence economy beside the cash economy in Tanganyika means that two forms of distribution co - exist: the commercial distribution system, consisting of whole - salers and retailers, and the local system of barter and pur - chase carried on mainly in the innumerable local markets, held usually at least once a week in all parts of the country. At these markets immediate surpluses of local produce as well as local handicrafts are bartered and sold. They extend the scope of the subsistence economy. If any one family cannot grow or make all its day -to -day requirements, it can obtain most of them by barter or purchase from local sources in the market. It is only when these local sources of supply are inadequate that people turn to the commercial distribution system for their needs.

Thus for a very large part of the population the commercial distribution system is merely supplementary to the indigenous system of production and barter. Buying goods in a shop is by no means their only source of supply, as in more advanced eco - nomies. It is in fact only made use of for comparatively excep - tional purchases, particularly of clothing, but also of such items

as soap, kerosene, cigarettes and patent medicines. The fact
that these purchases are comparatively exceptional can be
seen from the average purchasing power wielded by the African
population. The World Bank Mission estimated that in 1958
money incomes of the African population averaged very roughly
$16.8 per head. This figure may have increased to $18.2 by
1961. It covers the earnings of those in paid employment in
agriculture, industry, government and transport etc., and also
income from the sale of cash crops, which is heavily concentrated in certain areas where the major African cash crops of
cotton and coffee are grown, i.e. the Lake Region, Moshi-
Arusha, Bukoba and parts of the Southern Highlands. Throughout the rest of the country the cash earnings of about two-thirds
of the population probably do not average more than $5.6 a head
a year. Clearly this will not cover more than a very small
volume of purchases, especially as taxes also have to be paid
out of this sum. The significance and effect on the functioning
of the distribution system of this very low level of purchasing
power is considered in greater detail later in this report.

Seasonal nature of demand

A further very important factor affecting distribution in
Tanganyika is the extremely seasonal nature of demand. In
industrialised countries the demand for certain lines of goods
varies considerably according to the season, but since earnings
remain fairly constant throughout the year, overall demand
does not fluctuate very greatly. The biggest increase is normally at Christmas, when in the United Kingdom for the month
of December sales rise about 35 per cent above the level for the
rest of the year. In other months total sales do not vary by
more than about 10 per cent up or down. In Tanganyika a very
large part of total earnings is derived from the sale of agricultural produce, which in any one district is usually marketed
within a two or three month period each year. During these
months, which vary slightly from region to region, the value
of monthly sales is frequently double that of other months of the
year, and may in some instances go up to three or four times
the value. In many areas business comes virtually to a standstill in the out-of-season months.

Lack of homogeneity in the market

Yet another serious problem is the lack of homogeneity in
the market in Tanganyika. The three main communities,
African, Asian and European, with their different ways of life,
demand very different types of goods. There is, of course,
some overlapping, and this is increasing. With the total market already so small and spread over so large an area, this

further fragmentation adds considerably to the difficulties.

These are some of the more important factors, geographical, economic and social, which have shaped the distribution system in Tanganyika. They constitute the peculiar problems which the distribution system has been faced with, and has had to try to solve.

FUNCTIONS AND SCOPE
OF THE DISTRIBUTION SYSTEM

The purpose of a distribution system is to supply the consumer with what he wants in the right form, at the time and the place that he wants it. Wholesalers and retailers provide the link between the producer and the consumer. When, as in a more or less subsistence economy, these are not very far apart, the distribution system can be comparatively simple, a direct exchange between producers and consumers in a local market. When producers, through specialisation and the growth of manufacturing industry, grow further apart from consumers, both in time and space, then a more elaborate distribution network becomes necessary. This is particularly true in a country like Tanganyika where the change tends to be from a simple subsistence economy to one where primary products are being exported and most of the consumer's requirements, i.e. manufactured articles, are imported. Consumer and producer become at one jump about as far apart as they can be.

The purpose of a distribution system is fairly simple. The functions which it has to perform to fulfil this purpose are much more complex. The first and most obvious is to organise the transport of the goods from the producer to the consumer. But the "middleman" has numerous other functions also, including stockholding, forward purchasing, financing purchase and sales, levelling of price variations, bulk-breaking, if necessary repacking and finally creation of demand by good salesmanship. With some goods he may have to supply servicing and repair facilities. Clearly the middleman is performing, or should be performing, various functions which have to be undertaken by someone if goods are to be transferred efficiently from producer to consumer. Furthermore the middleman is taking a variety of risks which will be greater or smaller according to the type of goods he is dealing in and the circumstances in which he is trading. He runs the risk of variations in price, of changes in consumer tastes and fashions, of losses during storage, particu-

larly of perishable goods, and of losses and breakages during
transport. For all these he must be compensated.

The middleman in most countries is not popular and is very
often considered something of a parasite, taking his rake-off
without performing any useful function. This attitude is widely
prevalent in Tanganyika. However, as we have seen, the
middleman is in fact performing a variety of vital functions.
It would be useless for the producer to produce if his products
were not distributed to the consumers who are prepared to pay
for them. Clearly some middlemen perform their functions
more efficiently and cheaply than others, but this does not
mean that the role of the middlemen is parasitical. Without
him the whole economy would come to a grinding halt.

Two separate distribution systems operate side by side in
Tanganyika, the system of local markets and the commercial
system. It is the purpose of this report to study the second of
these. There are also two sides to the commercial distribu -
tion system. There is the part dealing with the marketing of
crops grown by farmers in Tanganyika, and there is the part
which distributes goods to the consumer, i.e. produce trading
and distributive trading. The two forms of trading are of
course interconnected, and in many instances both are carried
on by the same traders. However, it is not the purpose of this
study to examine the problems of produce trading. Several
crops grown in Tanganyika are entirely for export, and we are
not concerned with them. Some are partly for export and partly
for internal consumption while others are grown entirely for
internal consumption. It is not our purpose to examine here
how these crops are sold by the grower to the dealer, but once
the produce is in the hands of the wholesaler, we are concerned
with the problems of distribution to the consumer.

This division may seem somewhat artificial, but the subject
of produce marketing is an exceedingly complex one and would
require an entirely separate study. Though the problems of
produce marketing are not covered, the relationship between
produce trading and distributive trading, in so far as they are
carried on by the same persons, is examined in Chapter 3.

THE MARKET AND SOURCES OF SUPPLY

The market

Before attempting to analyse the structure of the distribution
system it is necessary to examine briefly, on the one hand, the

customers in Tanganyika and their requirements and, on the
other, the sources of supply of the goods distributed.

The population of Tanganyika was estimated to be 9.4
million in 1961. Of these, 9.25 million were Africans,
133,000 Asians and Arabs and 22,000 Europeans. Almost
all the African population lives in rural areas. In 1957, when
the last census was taken, there were 33 townships in Tanganyika, ranging in size from Dar es Salaam with a total population of 128,742 down to Lushoto with a total population of
1,270. Only 3.25 per cent of the African population lived in
these townships. On the other hand, most of the Asians and
Europeans live in the townships; in 1957, 72.5 per cent of the
Asians and Arabs and 40 per cent of the Europeans. In addition to the gazetted townships there are many minor settlements and trading centres. None of these is very large, though
a few are bigger than some of the smaller townships. Most of
the remaining 27.5 per cent of the Asian and Arab population
live in them, and some of the remaining 50 per cent of Europeans.

The population of the eleven largest towns in 1957 is given
below.

POPULATION OF THE PRINCIPAL
TOWNSHIPS, 1957

	African	Asian	European	Total
Dar es Salaam	93,363	30,900	4,479	128,742
Tanga	27,973	9,312	768	38,053
Mwanza	15,241	4,270	366	19,877
Tabora	12,005	3,016	340	15,361
Morogoro	12,440	1,784	281	14,507
Moshi	9,399	3,886	441	13,726
Dodoma	10,386	2,699	350	13,435
Ujiji	11,739	261	11	12,011
Mtwara	9,617	635	207	10,459
Lindi	8,370	1,845	100	10,315
Arusha	5,161	3,999	878	10,038
Total	215,694	62,609	8,221	286,524

Source Tanganyika Statistical Abstract 1961.

Since 1957 the total population of all these towns, except
Mtwara and perhaps Lindi, has almost certainly risen, particularly that of Dar es Salaam, though in 1962 the European
population of such places as Mwanza, Tabora, Dodoma and
Mtwara fell steeply. Other main centres of Asian population,
with more than 1,000 Asian and Arab inhabitants in 1957, were
Bukoba, Iringa, Musoma and Mbeya. Other centres of European population with over 200 Europeans were Iringa, Mbeya
and Lushoto.

The eleven towns listed contained only 2.5 per cent of the
total African population, but 61 per cent of all Asians and 40
per cent of all Europeans. The non-African population is thus
very highly urbanised, and the problem of distributing to it is
largely one of serving the main towns. This is clearly true of
the Asians, but in fact it is equally true of the Europeans, though
this does not appear from the figures above. Although only 40
per cent of the European population lived actually in the eleven
largest towns, a further 40 per cent lived within a radius of 50
miles of them and of three others, Iringa, Mbeya and Lushoto.
Ujiji can in fact be omitted. As almost all European families
have cars, they do the bulk of their shopping in these towns.

Most of the Africans who have comparatively high incomes
and westernised tastes live in the main towns. But the problem
of reaching the overwhelming mass of the African consumers
is one of distributing to a widely scattered rural population,
seldom grouped even into villages. This means that it is
usually necessary for the consumer to travel a considerable
distance to reach even one quite small shop. It may be necessary in many areas to travel at least 50 miles to reach a trading centre, let alone a township, though in the wealthier,
more densely populated areas it would be exceptional to have
to travel more than 15 to 20 miles.

The three main communities have very different patterns
of consumption, though of course their requirements tend increasingly to overlap and merge one into the other. A detailed
analysis of consumption pattern is outside the scope of this report, which is concerned with how the distribution system
functions, rather than with the goods which it handles. Nevertheless clearly the one affects the other.

Most Africans obtain most of their day-to-day requirements
outside the commercial distribution system, by growing them or
making them themselves or by bartering or buying them in the
local market. Only the comparatively small number who are in
full-time paid employment in towns or on estates buy all their
requirements from retailers. For most Africans, piecegoods and

cheap clothing, which they cannot produce themselves, form by far the most important part of their purchases; the next most important are staple foodstuffs or "ration goods" such as maize meal, rice, beans, sugar and salt.   These are of course more heavily consumed in towns, but are also consumed in most rural areas to supplement the local produce, particularly in the months before the harvest when local supplies run short.   Other major items of African consumption which are stocked in almost all small shops are cigarettes, soap, kerosene, tea, tinned milk, various types of cooking oils, matches, various patent medicines, razor blades, aluminium and enamelware, frequently biscuits, beads in certain areas, cotton thread, and writing materials.   In the towns, beer and soft drinks are important items.   In rural areas much of the sugar sold is for brewing pombe.

In the towns and trading centres where there is a sizable population receiving a regular cash income, there is a demand for a variety of foodstuffs, which differ from area to area and at different times of year, but which include wheat flour, sembe, dagaa (small dried fish), many varieties of peas and beans, millet, cassava, potatoes, onions, various vegetable oils, coffee, tinned baby food and a small selection of imported tinned foods.

Items which are bought only occasionally, but for which there is a relatively large demand, besides piecegoods and cheap clothing, are shoes, hoes, bicycles and spare parts, corrugated iron sheets, sewing machines, radios, cheap crockery and cutlery, padlocks, hurricane lamps, watches and radio batteries. These are normally only found in shops in towns or trading centres.

The demand for piecegoods varies very much from area to area, but there is a big demand for americani (grey unbleached cotton cloth), kaniki (black cotton cloth), khangas (printed cotton squares) khaki drill, and other cotton materials dyed in the piece, frequently black, vikoi (loin clothes with a coloured border), spun rayon printed materials and blankets of cotton or mixed cotton and wool.   Clothing, i.e. dresses, shirts, shorts etc., is normally made up by a tailor, usually employed at the retail shop. By far the biggest demand for ready-made clothing is for cheap shirts, followed by cheap knitwear, mainly vests, and other items such as shorts, handkerchiefs etc.   There is a demand also for second-hand clothing, mainly in the colder highland areas.

The items of all sorts listed above constitute a very large part indeed of the total purchases by African consumers.   Of course numerous other items are also bought, in fact the full range of consumer goods, but on the whole these constitute only occasional purchases, and by a comparatively small section of the African population. The demand for other items, therefore, is usually very small in any one area, and the turnover slow.

These remarks are generalisations covering the African market throughout Tanganyika, but generalisations of this sort can be misleading. It should not be forgotten that there is an enormous diversity of demand in the different districts. In the United Kingdom it is well knownthat there are appreciable differences between the market say in a London suburb, a town in Lancashire or a small town in the Highlands of Scotland. However, the differences in the market in Tanganyika are very much greater. The differences in climate between various parts of Tanganyika, in particular between the coast and the highland areas, are very great. There are very wide difference between the ways of life, traditions and cultures of people in different areas. Underlying all this it must be remembered that the goods supplied in the shops are in most cases only supplementing the goods, particularly foodstuffs, which are produced locally. These vary very much from district to district, so that what is required to supplement them also varies.

In a country such as the United Kingdom the differences between the market in different areas are mainly ones of taste, often produced by variations in the size of the different income groups. The basic requirements of the population are very simi lar throughout the country. In Tanganyika it is just the basic requirements which differ most, particularly with regard to foo but also as to clothing. Strangely, it is the slightly less basic requirements which are the most unvarying, such as cigarettes, kerosene, razor blades, soap, tea, aspirin and matches. There are great variations in the composition of the stock and the quan tities sold of such items as maize meal of various qualities, rice of various qualities, beans and peas of innumerable varieties, cottonseed, groundnut, simsim or coconut oils, this last not nor mally used for cooking but for toilet purposes, ghee, cassava, millet, groundnuts and dagaa.

Differences in clothing are equally marked. In some areas the demand is very heavy for kaniki or americani, in others for the kitenge or for khangas. If dresses are worn the demand may be more for plain colours or for printed materials for making up. For men the demand varies in different areas for vikoi, shukas, vests, material for khanzus, khaki drill for shorts or trousers, americani or various materials for shirts. Certain designs, particularly of khangas, will be popular in some areas but unsaleable in others. In the Central Regions check material are extremely popular, though there is little demand elsewhere. Also in the Central Region the demand is for the 42-inch kitenge, while in the Lake Region, where the people on the whole have more cash, only the 48-inch variety can be sold.

In the field of agricultural implements there are several different designs of hoes, and only certain designs can be sold in certain areas. There also tends to be considerable conservatism in the colours of paint bought in certain areas and by particular communities. There are parts of the country where the normal diet of the people is largely maize meal, which leads to a rather heavy demand for certain popular purgatives.

The demand for all these items naturally also varies enormously according to the season as well as the district, both because the availability of local produce and the availability of cash varies seasonally.

The Asian population is, as we have seen, highly urbanised. Asians normally have to buy all their requirements from shops in towns or trading centres. The range of basic foodstuffs bought does not differ very greatly from that bought by the African population. The main differences are no maize flour or cassava, more atta and wheat flour, ghee, onions, potatoes and other vegetables, dhal and, of course, spices as well as butter and milk. Unlike Europeans, the Asians buy very few tinned foods.

In piecegoods and clothing there is no demand from Asians for the stock African lines such as americani, kaniki, khangas, vikoi, plain black material or cheap spun rayon prints. Much of the clothing and materials used by the Asian community are Indian styles which come direct from India, particularly, of course, saris, and are not bought by any other communities. However, the type of clothing bought by Asians is becoming increasingly similar to that bought by Europeans.

Outside the ranges of food and clothing, the manufactured consumer goods bought by the three main communities do not differ greatly. Demand is not so much a question of race as of income, though of course tastes in design and styling differ to some extent, particularly in household items.

The pattern of consumption by the European community is practically the same as in Europe. Their consumption of tinned and, increasingly, of frozen foodstuffs is very heavy. The Europeans together with the wealthier section of the Asian community provide the main market for consumer durables, though the most rapidly expanding market is among the better-off Africans.

SOURCES OF SUPPLY

Goods passing through the commercial distribution system
in Tanganyika come from three sources: overseas, neighbouring East African territories and local production. Overseas
supplies are imported through the ports of Dar es Salaam,
Tanga, Lindi and Mtwara and through Mombasa in Kenya.
Kenya and Uganda supply manufactured goods and agricultural
produce across their respective borders. Local production is
both agricultural and manufacturing. Agricultural production
is very much the larger in total, but only a part enters the
commercial distribution system. Some agricultural products
are distributed unprocessed, but others are first milled or
otherwise processed. Local manufacturing in Tanganyika is
restricted to a comparatively small range of products, the
most important of which are cigarettes, beer, cotton textiles,
shoes, soap, soft drinks, bread, canned meat, and furniture.
Other items produced are knitwear, paint, aluminiumware,
razor blades, nails and ice-cream. The output of all these
industries is consumed locally, except the canned meat, much
of which is exported.

By aggregating these various sources of supply it is possible
to obtain a rough idea of the quantity and value of the different
goods distributed annually in Tanganyika, and it is useful to
record the totals under the main headings in order to have
some idea of the quantities handled by the various sections of
the distribution network.

Of the goods which were imported into Tanganyika in 1961,
$92.7 million worth, excluding government imports, were
classified as for net home consumption. Of this about $16.8
million worth was producers' capital goods, i.e. machinery of
all sorts, which are not normally handled by wholesalers and
retailers, but are either imported direct by the buyer or, more
usually, through a manufacturer's representative or agent.
There are also certain industrial fuels and raw materials
which are obtained direct from suppliers and cannot be said to
enter the commercial distribution system as such. The most
important items under this heading are fuel oils, aviation
spirit and yarn for textile weaving. This excludes a further
$3.5 million of imports from the commercial distribution sys-
tem. However, to the c.i.f. value of goods must be added the
import duty. Import duties on goods imported into Tanganyika
amounted to $22.1 million in 1961. Almost the whole of this

fell on goods entering the commercial distribution system, since producers' capital goods, fuels and raw materials are not subject to import duty.

The total value therefore of goods entering the commercial distribution system from overseas in 1961 was approximately $94.5 million.

The value of goods produced in Kenya and Uganda and recorded as being imported into Tanganyika in 1961 was $29.7 million. No duty is paid on these imports, and they consisted, with hardly any exceptions, of consumer goods which all entered the commercial distribution system.

It is extremely difficult to obtain reliable estimates of the volume or value of agricultural products which enter the commercial distribution system. Figures of production of locally consumed crops are based on estimates made by officers of the Agriculture Department. In addition to the problem of estimating production by hundreds of thousands of small producers all over the country, it is very difficult to assess how much is consumed by the growers, how much traded in the local markets and how much passes through the hands of produce dealers and wholesalers.

The main agricultural products which enter the distribution system are rice, maize, cottonseed oil, sugar, groundnut oil, cassava, beans and pulses, wheat, millet and onions. There are also a great many minor crops. The best estimate of the value of this locally grown agricultural produce entering the distribution system in 1961, after being processed, is about $21.0 million.

Of the manufactures produced in Tanganyika, the two most important, beer and cigarettes, are excisable, so that accurate figures for the value of production are available. Figures for the other industries are of varying reliability. The value of goods manufactured in Tanganyika which entered the commercial distribution system in 1961 was probably about $14 million. This figure includes a large element of excise duty on beer and cigarettes manufactured in Kenya and Uganda but consumed in Tanganyika.

It would seem from these calculations that about $159.6 million worth of goods entered the distribution system in 1961.

GENERAL ASPECTS OF DISTRIBUTION
IN TANGANYIKA

The background to the problems of distribution in Tanganyika has been outlined above; before embarking on a detailed analysis, a brief general description of the commercial distribution system is given below.

Historical developments

The distribution system in Tanganyika one hundred years ago consisted of thousands of small local markets, in which local produce was bartered, supplemented in some areas by Arab traders dealing mainly in slaves and ivory, which they bartered in return for piecegoods, beads, metal implements and a small selection of cheap manufactured articles. Except in the coastal areas, where Arab and Asian traders were beginning to be esta blished, there were no permanent shops of any sort. With the establishment of German rule and the building of the railway at the end of the last century trade began to spread gradually inlan It was still entirely in the hands of non-Africans. The importin firms were mainly, though not exclusively, European, while the smaller wholesalers and retailers were Asian and Arab.

Trade spread as plantations, mainly of sisal, were establish thus creating a market among the paid African estate workers, and as the marketing of various cash crops by African growers increased in volume. The purchase of produce was almost en tirely in the hands of Asians and Arabs, and the normal pattern of trade in the interior was for a small duka to be established to sell imported goods, mainly piecegoods, and to buy the local pr duce from the growers. Shops were also established at the vari centres where there were European farmers, administrative off cers or missionaries.

To begin with trade was almost entirely a question of selling imported manufactures and buying and exporting local produce. But as communications improved, the trade in agricultural sur- pluses between different areas increased until an East African- wide network was built up. To-day East Africa, taken as a whol is almost completely self-supporting in foodstuffs, except in famine years. A later development, mainly since 1946, has bee the growth of the trade in East African manufactured goods, lar from Kenya, but also local and from Uganda.

Africans began to enter the retail trade as shopkeepers in re latively large numbers in the inter-war years. Those who were able to save a small sum, either from the sale of cash crops or of earnings from paid employment, set up small dukas, usually the more remote areas, where there was no direct competition from Asian or Arab shopkeepers. Another process was for Asia to set up branch shops, managed by Africans. These also were away from the trading centres and minor settlements, to which t Asians were restricted, and their main purpose was to tap large supplies of local produce. The African in charge of the branch bought the local produce of the areas as well as carrying on a retail business.

The big increase in the number of African shops, however, has taken place in the last ten to fifteen years. Unfortunately no figures are available for the earlier years, but by 1959 there were 36, 157 African retailers licensed; in 1961 the figure apparently fell to 34, 581 but this may have been due to incomplete returns from two or three districts. In 1953 an estimate based on incomplete returns put the number of licensed African retailers at about 27, 000. In 1945 there were probably less than half this number. Very few of these African shops are in towns or trading centres; almost all are situated in the interior.

Originally, as we have seen, the import-export trade in Tanganyika was mainly in the hands of the Arabs, though there were also Asians trading from very early times. In 1863 there were already estimated to be between 5, 000 and 6, 000 Asians in Zanzibar and on the East African mainland. These were almost entirely engaged in trade, mostly between East Africa and the Far East. However, with the coming of colonial rule, first German, then British, most of the import-export trade passed into the hands of European firms, which had the contacts with suppliers and markets in Europe, though the trade with India and the Far East was still mainly conducted by Asians. The European firms were frequently branches or subsidiaries of trading companies with wide interests, and had access to outside sources of finance. Thus the European firms tended to provide capital and perhaps a certain amount of technical know-how. A few had, and still have, branches up-country, but these have never been very numerous or extensive in their coverage.

Asian traders normally, though not always, bought their supplies from European importers, and sold the produce they had purchased to European exporters. The Asian traders were prepared to subsist at a very much lower standard of living than the Europeans, and were therefore able to trade in areas where the turnover was small. Asian, and to a lesser extent Arab traders, performed an invaluable service in the development of the economy of Tanganyika by widening the market, increasing the scope of the cash economy and bringing trade to areas which otherwise would have had to wait for decades to be opened up. They performed this task at a time when no one else was ready or able to perform it. No European traders were prepared to carry on a business in such remote areas and with such a small turnover, while at that time there were very few Africans who had the experience or the money to open and operate successfully a small shop. It is worth noting that in Rhodesia, where it was the official policy to keep Asians out of trade as much as possible, the

development of the rural areas, away from the areas of European settlement, was, and is, very much behind the development of the rural areas in East Africa. Where there have been
no Asian traders to open shops, buy the local produce and sell
imported goods, no one else has come forward to perform these
functions. The rural areas have been almost completely without shops, and only recently have Africans themselves begun
to trade on any significant scale.

In West Africa the import-export trade and much of the distribution system were long dominated by four or five very large
trading concerns, which have operated in many cases to reduce
competition. In Nigeria, for instance, the United Africa Company Limited and its subsidiaries imported 34 per cent of all
commercial imports in 1949, while the five next largest companies imported a further 24 per cent of the total. There is
nothing comparable with this in Tanganyika or East Africa as a
whole. There is no one large firm nor any group of firms
which dominates the import or export trade of Tanganyika. The
largest single importer in Tanganyika does not import as much
as 5 per cent by value of the total imports from overseas.

This contrast between East and West Africa is due to various
mainly historical, factors, one of the most important of which
was the predominance of mercantile considerations in the development of European links with West Africa. When the scram-
ble for Africa began, Europe had already been trading with the
coastal regions of West Africa for centuries; European commercial interest in East Africa was, however, not stimulated
until after the opening of the Suez canal, by which time Arab
traders were well-established. In West Africa the large,
heavily capitalised, European import houses have until recently
operated an extensive network of wholesale and retail establish-
ments, distributing imported goods and buying local produce.
In East Africa the European import-export houses have always
been able to distribute their imports to, and purchase the local
produce for export from, the Asian traders. They have not
wished, and in most cases in fact have been unable, to compete
with the Asian traders at the semi-wholesale and retail levels.

Recent developments

The roles of the different intermediaries in the distribution
system in Tanganyika have been changing considerably in recent
years. Starting at the lower end of the distribution chain, there
has been the rise of the small African duka, mainly in the rural
areas. Parallel with this has been the growth of the co-operativ
movement, which has taken over a large part of the purchasing
of local produce. These two trends have caused the Asian retail

to retreat from the outlying districts and smaller rural
centres, and concentrate more in the townships and trading
centres. There are still many thousands of small Asian and
Arab retailers, but an increasing number are trying to set up
as sub-wholesalers, supplying in small wholesale quantities
to African shopkeepers.

Further up the chain, as the more successful Asian wholesalers and import-export merchants have expanded their
business, so they have more and more invaded the field which
used to be the preserve of the European general import -
export houses.

In the inter-war years most goods were imported by European firms and many of the lines were agency lines. Now the
trade is much more open and most of the bulk lines for the
African market, in particular piecegoods, are imported by
Asian firms. The European general importers are becoming
much less general, and are handling an increasingly specialised range. Today European firms deal mainly in industrial
machinery, agricultural machinery and implements, pharma-
ceutical products and chemicals. Cars, building materials,
hardware and consumer durables are imported by both European and Asian firms, while piecegoods, clothing, groceries
and provisions are mainly handled by Asian firms.

Lack of clear-cut division between wholesalers and retailers

There is no clear-cut distinction between importers,
wholesalers, sub-wholesalers and retailers in Tanganyika.
Most importers are also wholesalers and very often retailers
as well. Only a few of the largest wholesalers do not also
sell retail, and all sub-wholesalers sell goods in retail quantities. This aspect of the distribution system is discussed in
more detail later in this report, but it is important when look-
ing at the general picture of distribution to realize how the various stages of the distributive process merge one into the other.

The position of import houses

Imported commercial supplies reach Tanganyika through
European and Asian import merchants. Of the overseas suppliers or manufacturers, only the oil companies maintain local
depots, from which they supply in wholesale quantities. A few
manufacturers have their own representatives permanently in
the country, but these are attached to local import houses. For
capital goods and machinery of all kinds there are manufacturers' representatives, who do not carry stocks, so that orders
placed with them are normally executed by the overseas principals. Some of these representatives have their head offices
in Nairobi and Mombasa, through which their orders are passed.

None of the European or Asian import-export houses has a very widespread distribution network in Tanganyika. There are four European-owned firms and one Asian firm which can still be described as general importers, though they are tending to cut down the number of their lines and increase their degree of specialisation. Two of these have eight branches in Tanganyika two have six and one has four. Their Tanganyika head offices are all in Dar es Salaam. They all have branches also in Tanga and Mwanza, four have branches in Lindi and four in Mtwara, three have branches in Moshi and two in Dodoma. The other more specialised importers do not have more than three or four branches each, with the exception of the motor distributors.

The import houses, though they mostly carry out all the functions of importer, wholesaler and retailer, do this from the same premises or from only a few branches. They do not have a network of wholesale branches supplying in turn to a network of retail branches, which used to be the system common in West Africa.

Inter-territorial trade

It is not necessary to be a licensed importer in order to import goods from Kenya and Uganda, so that there is a tendency for more wholesalers, especially in the north of the country, to handle imports from the other East African territories than handle those from overseas. Otherwise the pattern is not very different. One or two of the larger manufacturers in Kenya and Uganda have their own depots in Tanganyika. Other producers in Kenya and Uganda have appointed agents in Tanganyika, for instance for cement, metal doors and windows, textiles, soap, cooking fats etc., to mention the more important. In many items the trade is completely open, particularly in agricultural produce.

The most highly organised and tightly controlled distribution networks are those of the biggest local manufacturers, in particular of cigarettes, beer, tea and shoes. The manufacturers of these items do a large part of their own distribution, but never the whole of it, as they have to rely on the multitude of small shops scattered over the country to give their products the widest possible coverage.

The importance of wholesaling and retailing functions in
                                                    Tanganyika

There are two striking features of the present distribution system in Tanganyika. With the exception of the four products mentioned above, manufacturers have scarcely entered the field of distribution at all. The business of distribution is still performed almost entirely by independent wholesalers and retailers. The second feature, which is closely connected with the first, is the very important role played by the wholesaler, and the relatively enormous number of wholesalers that are operating in Tanganyika.

In the industrialised countries of Western Europe and America the traditional distribution system, and in particular the position of the wholesaler in it, has been eroded from both ends over the last fifty years or so. The retailer's role has been reduced by such innovations as self-service stores, mail order trading and direct selling. However, the wholesaler's role has been even more seriously hit. Chain stores, co-operative stores, multiples and department stores have all grown up and have been able to undertake large-scale purchasing direct from the manufacturer, by-passing the wholesaler altogether. At the manufacturing end, large-scale mass-production industries have evolved, generating a pressure for ever-increasing sales. The most usual means of achieving this has been to develop brand names, back the branded goods with heavy advertising and adopt a fixed price policy. The manufacturer creates the sales demand and takes over the distribution to the retailer in order to reap the full benefit. Amalgations and mergers tend to increase the range of branded goods manufactured by one company, and the company develops its own distribution network. The next step is to acquire a string of retail outlets. Sometimes the reverse process takes place, and a chain store organisation acquires its own manufacturing enterprises.

In the United States by 1939 only 26.5 per cent of manufactured goods were distributed through wholesalers. By 1948 only 1.5 per cent of clothing sales passed through wholesale channels. It would be hard to find a more extreme contrast to the situation in Tanganyika today. The wholesaler in Tanganyika still plays a very important role. This is due to the entirely different circumstances which prevail.

There are few manufacturers in East Africa, and only one or two could be described as mass-producing. Manufactured goods are mostly imported from abroad and therefore have to be distributed by importers and wholesalers. The market is small and spread over a huge area. It is impossible, except for a very few products, mainly patent medicines, and at considerable expense, to distribute direct to the retailer. Very few of the goods sold to the African consumers are branded lines, and effective advertising to such a widely scattered rural population, many of whom are illiterate, is difficult. These are some of the factors which make the wholesale function essential, and ensure that this func-

tion will have to be carried out by some agency or other for
many years to come.

The degree of specialisation in retailing and wholesaling

A very noticeable characteristic of the distribution system
in Tanganyika is the almost complete lack of any specialisation
as between different types of retail trades. It has been suggeste
that there is a cycle of evolution in the retail trade. To begin
with most of the retail trade is carried out by the general store,
which aims at providing practically everything in common use.
With larger markets a degree of specialisation develops. But
then the revolution comes full-cycle. Large department stores
and supermarkets appear, stocking almost the full range of goo
under one roof. This has been the pattern in Western Europe a
America. Tanganyika's retail trade is only in the first stage of
this process of evolution at present, though it is beginning now t
enter the second stage. There is undoubtedly a trend towards
greater specialisation. As yet it has not gone far.

Specialised retail shops, which can be described as, for
instance, grocers, ironmongers, chemists, clothing shops, boo
sellers and so on, are confined almost entirely to the larger
towns, particularly where there is a sizable European populatio
i.e. Dar es Salaam, Tanga, Arusha and Mwanza. Other towns
where the process has begun are Moshi, Iringa, Mbeya, Lushot
Morogoro, Dodoma and Tabora. Outside these places there are
very few specialized shops indeed, and even in them there are
not more than one to two hundred altogether, many of these bein
in Dar es Salaam.

In the wholesale trade, as might be expected, there is rather
more specialisation, the main categories being piecegoods, pro
duce, groceries and provisions, clothing and fancy goods, hardware and building materials, cutlery and sundries and electrical
goods. There are also various rather more specialised trades,
such as the motor trade, machinery, bicycles and chemist good
which are sometimes carried on on their own, particularly the
first. Even in the broad categories listed above, there are com
paratively few wholesalers who deal in only one of the lines. Sor
of the bigger wholesalers in the main towns and a good many qui
small wholesalers in Dar es Salaam do specialise. Most deal i
at least two lines, often more, though they usually have one or t
principal lines, the others being of minor importance.

Geographical aspects of distribution

When considering the routes taken by goods being distributed
across the country, it is essential to remember that the three
East African territories form a free trade area and that their di
tribution systems cannot be viewed separately. They are highl

interdependent. In particular, much of Tanganyika's distribution network is really part of the Kenya network, based on Mombasa and Nairobi. A large part of Tanganyika's imported supplies come through Mombasa. Besides the considerable volume
of manufactured goods coming into Tanganyika from Kenya and
Uganda, there is also a large inter-territorial trade in local
produce.

Imported goods. Of the goods imported into Tanganyika from
abroad, just under a quarter, i.e. 24 per cent by value, passed
through Mombasa in 1961. In fact a large part of northern Tanganyika receives most of its imported supplies via Mombasa.
A glance at the map will show that the Moshi-Arusha area, and
indeed the whole Northern Region, falls within the natural market area of Mombasa. The direct rail and road connection is
much shorter than to the smaller and less well-equipped port of
Tanga. Tanga Region itself obtains a sizable proportion of its
imported supplies by road from Mombasa.

The Lake and West Lake Regions also obtain a very large
part of their imported supplies through Mombasa. Probably
over half of the imports into the Lake Region, and between 75
and 80 per cent of the imports into the West Lake Region come
via Mombasa. Supplies come up the railway line in Kenya as far
as Kisumu, and are then shipped by Lake steamer to the ports of
Bukoba, Mwanza and Musoma in Tanganyika. The freight rates
charged by East African Railways and Harbours on the two routes,
Mombasa to Kisumu and Dar es Salaam to Mwanza, have been
equalised as far as Bukoba is concerned, but are 22 per cent
cheaper to Musoma via Mombasa and Kisumu. The rates to
Mwanza direct by rail from Dar es Salaam are slightly cheaper
than by rail and steamer through Mombasa and Kisumu. The
difference is only 5 per cent however, and for many imports this
small difference in freight is not enough to cancel out the various
other advantages of obtaining supplies from Mombasa rather than
from Dar es Salaam.

Most of the supplies imported from abroad into the Northern,
Lake and West Lake Regions, therefore, come via Mombasa.
These regions contain a little over one-third of the total population of Tanganyika, and about the same proportion of its purchasing power.

76 per cent by value of imports from overseas entered Tanganyika in 1961 through the ports of Dar es Salaam, Tanga, Lindi
and Mtwara.   Dar es Salaam is by far the most important of
these. 84 per cent by weight of the goods imported direct into
Tanganyika came through Dar es Salaam, 12 per cent through
Tanga and 2 per cent each through Lindi and Mtwara.

The port of Tanga serves the region of the same name,
though most of Pare District obtains it supplies from Moshi,
and thus ultimately from Mombasa. Lindi and Mtwara serve
the Southern Region. They do not serve beyond its borders.
However, much of the supplies entering Lindi and Mtwara are
trans-shipped from Dar es Salaam, and in the dry season a
large part of these supplies come south by road instead of by
sea.

Dar es Salaam is of course the port for and terminus of the
Central Railway Line. As far as imported goods are concerned
it serves the whole of the Eastern, Western and Southern Highlands Regions and almost all the Central Region. The Lake and
Southern Regions obtain a large part of their imported supplies
through Dar es Salaam and West Lake Region a very small part.
Slightly over 60 per cent by value of Tanganyika's imports pass
through Dar es Salaam; this means about $59 million worth of
commercial imports in 1961. It is interesting to compare this
with the volume of imports through Mombasa. The comparable
figure was $259.0 million. Of this $37.2 million were direct
imports into Uganda, not handled by Mombasa merchants. No
doubt a large part of the remaining $221.8 million was imported
direct by Nairobi and other up-country Kenya merchants. Likewise some part of the imports through Dar es Salaam were imported direct by up-country merchants, though almost certainly
not as high a proportion as for Mombasa. But after these factors have been taken into account, it seems fairly certain that
the value of imported goods handled by Mombasa importers and
wholesalers is at least three times greater than that handled by
Dar es Salaam importers and wholesalers.

Goods manufactured in Kenya are imported into Tanganyika
by road or by rail and sea. Goods from Uganda normally cross
Lake Victoria by steamer and if necessary come down the railway from Mwanza.

Local products. The trade in local produce inside East Africa i
extremely complex. It depends to a great extent on which areas
have surpluses and which have shortages of the various food
crops in any particular year. However, there are certain areas
which produce fairly regular surpluses, and others which provide a fairly regular market for them. Kenya supplies to Tanga
yika large quantities of wheat, both milled and unmilled, also te
meat, butter and cottonseed oil. Uganda also supplies cottonsee
oil. Tanganyika sends to Kenya onions, beans, peas and pulses
and coconut oil, this last also to Uganda.

Inside Tanganyika the Lake Region regularly has a surplus of
cottonseed oil, the Moshi District of sugar, both the Rufiji Distr

in the Eastern Region and Rungwe District in Southern Highlands of rice, Southern Region of cassava, beans and peas, Northern Region also of beans and peas, much of it sent to Kenya, and of wheat. The Ufipa District of Western Region normally exports millet to other areas. The Tabora and Nzega Districts in the Western Region and the Nachingwea District in the Southern Region export groundnuts and groundnut oil. Surpluses of maize occur in varying quantities in different districts in different years. The main exporting areas are normally Northern Region, Southern Highlands, particularly the Iringa District, and Western Region, mainly Kasulu, Mpanda, Ufipa and Nzega Districts.

These surpluses of produce give rise to various regular trading arrangements, such as sugar from Moshi to Rungwe District with a return load of rice, or sugar again from Moshi to Mwanza with a return load of cottonseed oil. The produce wholesalers play a vital role in marketing surplus produce. It is as a result of this extensive trade in produce between regions that Tanganyika is able to be almost entirely self-sufficient in foodstuffs. Imports of foodstuffs from overseas form only a very small proportion of total imports; only 7 per cent of commercial imports in 1961, by far the largest items being sugar and tinned milk, between them forming over 60 per cent of all imports of foodstuffs. All the staple foodstuffs consumed are produced in East Africa. Shortly, when the Kilombero sugar scheme comes into full production, Tanganyika will be self-sufficient in sugar also.

Self-sufficiency of this sort can only be achieved if the distribution network is reasonably efficient. If the production of cash crops for local consumption is to be encouraged successfully, there must be the distribution system available to market the crops wherever there is a demand for them in East Africa. This requires a great many produce dealers up and down the country with considerable knowledge and experience. Most of these crops are food crops and perishable, so that errors of judgement in marketing can be serious. A wide knowledge of sources of supply, markets and transport facilities, not for just one crop, but for a great many, is required. A produce dealer in Arusha may be buying maize and cottonseed oil from Uganda, coconut oil from Tanga, rice from Tukuyu and groundnut oil from Nzega. He is buying these different types of produce partly for sale in the Arusha area, but also for sale in other areas, for instance coconut oil from Tanga in Uganda, so that he can obtain two-way loads for his transport. The dealer, therefore, has to have up-to-date knowledge of the constantly changing supply and demand position in many areas for a variety of crops.

It is through the medium of these merchants that the producer

is able to market his crops over the widest possible area and
the consumer is able to obtain supplies from all the available
sources. For these reasons it is in everyone's interest to encourage the development of this produce trading network on the
most efficient lines. In particular, so far as government action
is concerned, this means placing as few impediments in the way
of the trade as possible. Restrictions imposed by government
at present take two main forms, restrictions on the export from
particular districts or regions of produce which is thought to be
in short supply and, secondly, restrictions on the use of private
road transport.

The "East Africa Royal Commission, 1953-55", devoted a
section of its Report to the subject of restrictions on the export
of produce from the districts or regions in which it is grown.

The customary methods of production are based essentially
upon the notion of self-sufficiency in food supplies. One
result has been that the governments of East Africa have frequently had to institute famine relief measures in particular
areas. It is not surprising, therefore, that these governments should endeavour to prevent the occurrence of food
shortage. But in the policies which they have adopted they
have been unduly influenced by the fears and practices of the
indigenous populations, and by encouraging district and
regional self-sufficiency they have perpetuated the cause of
the evil which their measures were intended to combat,
namely the system of self-sufficiency itself. In their anxiety
to achieve security in the matter of food supplies they have
tended to regard the ordinary mechanism of the market as an
obstacle to the solution of their difficulties rather than as a
solvent of the problem. Instead of encouraging specialisation
and the free sale of surplus production of food and other agricultural products in suitable areas, in order to even out
shortages in other areas by the use of the normal machinery
of the market, government policy has frequently looked upon
the normal functioning of the market with suspicion. At
various times and in various districts it has discouraged
African producers from marketing food surpluses beyond the
limits of particular regions, or even of particular districts,
lest a food shortage should occur at some later date. But the
effects of the system of district self-sufficiency are not in
doubt. It perpetuates the vicious circle in which all subsistence economy moves, owing to the absence of those wider
markets which alone can ensure that a crop failure in one area
can be overcome by attracting supplies from further afield.

These comments, written in 1955, are equally true today. In fairness it must be said that it has been government policy for some years now to encourage the growing of cash crops, and for farmers to break away from the system of subsistence farming. However, when it comes to the point where local shortages are threatened, restrictions on the movement of produce are swiftly introduced. The purpose of these restrictions is to prevent growers from selling their crops for cash at harvest-time, running short of food later in the year and then having to buy food-stuffs at very much higher prices. This is of course an extremely paternalistic approach, it runs counter to the policy of breaking away from subsistence agriculture and it means that the growers never learn how a market economy operates. If progress is to be made, it cannot unfortunately always be made painlessly.

Restrictions on the use of private transport are not so serious or widespread. They occur mainly in the Southern Highlands, where certain concerns have a statutory monopoly of the transport of certain types of goods. This undoubtedly obstructs the free flow of produce at the cheapest rates across the country, but these restrictions are likely to come to an end shortly.

There are, in fact, certain positive steps which could be taken to facilitate the trade in produce and improve its efficiency, thus benefiting both producer and consumer. One of the greatest problems for the trader in Tanganyika is the lack of reliable information about crop production in different areas, and the failure to make the existing information as widely known as possible. Every effort should be made to ensure that as accurate forecasts as possible of crop-production by districts are obtained and then publicised over the radio and in the press. Prices of produce in different areas should also be publicised by all available means. This not only helps the traders, but is also one of the most effective means of ensuring that growers get fair prices.

As complete and accurate market information as possible is essential for the efficient functioning of a distribution system. Unreliable and incomplete information inevitably produces extreme fluctuations in price, coupled with local shortages or surpluses. Formerly inadequate communications were one of the main problems. Now as roads are being improved lack of market information is emerging as a major hindrance to efficient trading.

Another step which perhaps is worth considering at this stage would be the setting up of some form of produce exchange or series of exchanges. In this way trading between different areas can be greatly facilitated and market information can be much more quickly spread.

CHAPTER **3** THE STRUCTURE
OF THE
DISTRIBUTION SYSTEM

THE NUMBER AND LOCATION
OF WHOLESALERS AND RETAILERS

Detailed information concerning the number and location of
the different types of distributors by districts is available from
the trading licence returns. All traders have to be licensed,
and each different type of trader has to take out a different category of licence. The traders with whom we are concerned are
divided into four main categories, wholesalers, non-African
retailers, African retailers and itinerant traders. The first
two categories are sub-divided further. There are three types
of wholesaler's licence. Wholesalers are licensed to import and
export goods, import only or merely carry on a wholesale business. These are all further split into "the principal or only
place of business" and "subsidiary places of business". Separat
returns are shown for commission agents or manufacturers' representatives and brokers. Non-African retailers are sub-
divided into those who are licensed to import from abroad, split
again between principal and subsidiary places of business, those
licensed to buy produce from African growers, this licence in-
cludes a licence to carry on a retail business if it be so desired,
and finally those licensed merely to carry on the business of
retailing. The categories of African retailers and itinerant
traders are not sub-divided.

The table on pages 34-35 shows these licence figures by
Regions for the licensing year April 1, 1960 to March 31, 1961.
A more detailed breakdown of the figures by Districts is given ir
Appendix.   The charts on pages 38-42 show the distribution of
wholesalers and retailers, both African and non-African by distr

From observation and inquiry it seems that these licensing f
gures are surprisingly complete. Very few traders appear to ri
doing business without a licence although this varies somewhat f
district to district. Even the smaller shops in the more remote
areas normally have a licence, though clearly there are some wl
operate without. Generally, however, unlicensed shops are ver
small. It also seems likely that a good many hawkers operate
without an itinerant traders' license, but these are of only minor

importance.
Analysis by race
Trade licensing is still to some extent on a racial basis,
since non-African retailers have to pay more for their licence
than African retailers, and are recorded separately. All
wholesalers, of whatever race, have to obtain the appropriate
category of licence in order to carry on business. In fact there
is only a handful of African wholesalers. Almost all the wholesalers in Tanganyika are Asian, together with a small number
of Europeans.

Of the non-African retailers, a handful are Europeans; the
rest are Asian, Arab and Somali. No distinction is made in the
returns between these three racial groups, but some estimates
of their numbers can be made. The 1957 census showed that
4,326 Arabs were engaged in the wholesale and retail trade.
This was 74 per cent of all gainfully occupied Arabs. With the
increase in the Arab population in the four subsequent years,
the numbers engaged in trade probably rose to about 5,800 in
1961. A good many of these were certainly itinerant traders,
some were also employees, though most Arab shops are one-
man businesses, often with help from various unpaid family
workers. As a very rough estimate it can be said that there
were probably 2,500 Arab shops in Tanganyika in 1961, most of
them retailers, though some of them wholesalers, usually on a
comparatively small scale.

There were, in 1957, 732 Somalis recorded as engaged in
wholesale and retail trade. By 1961 this figure had probably
risen to about 900. Most of these Somalis are cattle traders,
but some own shops also, though these probably did not number
more than 100 at the outside.

From these calculations we see that the racial breakdown of
the non-African traders was as follows in 1961: there were
3,921 wholesalers, of whom the great majority were Asians,
though a small number of, on the whole, the larger concerns
were European and a small number of, on the whole, the
smaller concerns were Arab. There were 10,090 non-African
retail businesses of which about 7,500 were Asian and about
2,500 were Arab and Somali.

It should be remembered, however, when making these dis-
tinctions between wholesalers and retailers, that a trader licensed to carry on a wholesale business is permitted to do
business as a retailer as well, though not vice versa. There
are comparatively few wholesalers in Tanganyika who do not
also sell retail direct to the consumer. Some of the large wholesalers in the main towns do a purely wholesale business, but

TRADING LICENCES

Type of Licence		Dar es Salaam	Eastern Region	Central Region	Southern Highlands Region
Wholesaler (import	(i)	231	5	5	10
and export)	(ii)	28	4	4	1
Wholesaler (import	(i)	507	7	44	79
only)	(ii)	15	6	2	3
Wholesale only	(i)	356	190	84	177
	(ii)	16	47	8	12
Commission agent or manufacturer's representative		48	-	-	4
Broker		52	-	-	-
Total wholesalers		1,253	259	147	286
Non-African retailer(i) (including import) (ii)		82 7	2 -	12 1	17 1
Non-African produce buyer (incl. retailer)		48	602	570	272
Non-African retailer only		1,338	517	429	325
Total non-African retailers		1,475	1,121	1,012	615
Total wholesalers and non-African retailers		2,728	1,380	1,159	901
African retailers		230	4,157	2,088	3,671
Total traders (excl. itinerant)		2,958	5,537	3,247	4,572
Itinerant traders		53	763	579	783

(i). Principal place of business.
(ii). Subsidiary place of business.

BY REGIONS, 1960-61

West Lake Region	Lake Region	Tanga Region	Western Region	Northern Region	Southern Region	Tanganyika
10	24	19	32	34	26	396
4	24	33	11	5	28	142
32	206	121	80	145	43	1,264
6	34	32	6	13	13	130
32	241	86	181	43	165	1,555
3	17	12	19	6	124	264
-	2	2	-	3	-	59
-	1	1	-	-	-	54
87	549	306	329	249	399	3,864
20	80	42	2	114	5	376
1	2	2	-	20	6	40
116	647	177	636	243	358	3,669
197	914	1,144	440	423	278	6,005
334	1,643	1,365	1,078	800	647	10,090
421	2,192	1,671	1,407	1,049	1,041	13,954
2,798	7,820	3,893	4,322	2,396	3,206	34,581
3,219	10,012	5,564	5,729	3,445	4,247	48,535
1,655	1,410	3,112	1,113	1,611	497	11,576

General Notes: The licensing year runs from April 1, 1960 to March 31, 1961. The figures for the District of Nachingwea

most are also prepared to sell in retail quantities. In the
smaller townships, minor settlements and trading centres,
many of the Asian and Arab traders are mainly retailers, but
they are also doing a wholesale business in so far as they are
selling goods in very small wholesale lots to other shopkeepers,
mainly African, who are re-selling these goods to the consumer
This in fact, and under the trade licensing laws, is a whole -
saling operation and requires a wholesaler's licence.

   No real distinction is feasible between wholesalers and retailers in Tanganyika. The two categories merge gradually the
one into the other, though for the purposes of licensing there
has to be a sharp distinction. What happens in fact is that re -
tailers who only occasionally, and sometimes hardly ever, conduct any wholesale business, tend to take out a wholesale licenc
just to cover themselves. On the other hand the reverse proces
also undoubtedly takes place, and some retailers who do a sub -
stantial amount of small-scale wholesaling possess only a retail
licence.

   Traders who take out a licence to "purchase native produce
for resale in the Territory" are also permitted to carry on busi
ness as retailers on the same licence. Almost all of them do so
There are very few traders indeed with a permanent place of
business who confine their operations to buying local produce fo
resale. A licence of this type is really a retail licence which
also permits the retailer to buy local produce from the growers.

   The total number of wholesalers and non-African retailers

---

in the Southern Region and for the sub-district of Mbozi are not
available, so that the returns for the previous licensing period
have been used.   Likewise the returns for the Districts of
Tunduru, Southern Region, Mbulu, Northern Region, and
Kahama, Western Region, are incomplete, so that again the
returns of the previous licensing period have been used.   This
should affect the figures very little, as changes are only slight
from year to year.   There was, however, a sharp drop in
African trading licenses in the Moshi district, Northern Region,
and Rungwe District, Southern Highlands Region, in each
case to about half the previous year's figures. No explanation
for this is available.

Source Tanganyika Ministry of Finance.

taken together was 13, 954 in 1961. This in effect represents
the total number of non-African traders doing business in Tanganyika, since the number of African wholesalers is negligible.

The total number of African retailers licensed in 1961 was
34, 581. This was a drop of almost 1, 500 compared with the
licences issued in 1960, but this fall may have been due to incomplete returns from the Moshi and Rungwe districts, where
most of the decline took place.

There were in 1961 exactly two and a half times as many
African traders licensed as non-African traders. It is clearly
untrue therefore to say, as is often said, that the wholesale
and retail trade of Tanganyika is entirely in the hands of non-
Africans, particularly of Asians. Numerically the African
traders far out-number Asians and Arabs. It is, however,
true that the wholesale trade is almost entirely in the hands of
Asians, and it is also true, as we shall see later, that though
the Asian traders are less numerous than the African, they
handle, even at the retail level, much the greater part of the
business. In other words the average turnover of the Asian
and Arab retailers and of the wholesalers who are also doing a
retail business is very much higher than the average turnover
of the African retailers.

Wholesalers

From the figures of trading licences issued in 1961 contained
in the table above, it emerges very clearly that Dar es Salaam
is both the chief port and commercial centre of Tanganyika.
Almost a third of all the wholesalers in the country, and just
under one half of all the import-export merchants are located
there. After Dar es Salaam the largest number of wholesalers
is to be found in the Lake Region, followed by the Southern and
Western Regions. The smallest numbers are in West Lake and
Central Regions with only 87 and 147 wholesalers each. West
Lake has the smallest population of any of the regions and the
second lowest average monetary income. The lowest is the
Central Region. These two regions have the lowest total
monetary income of any of the regions.

The Lake Region, with the largest number of wholesalers
after Dar es Salaam, is also the region with the largest population and the largest total monetary income. The Southern and
Western Regions also have large populations, though not particularly high total monetary incomes. The relatively large number of wholesalers is probably due to the fact that both these
regions cover a very large area - they are the first and second
largest regions - their populations are scattered and they have
more townships and trading centres within their boundaries than

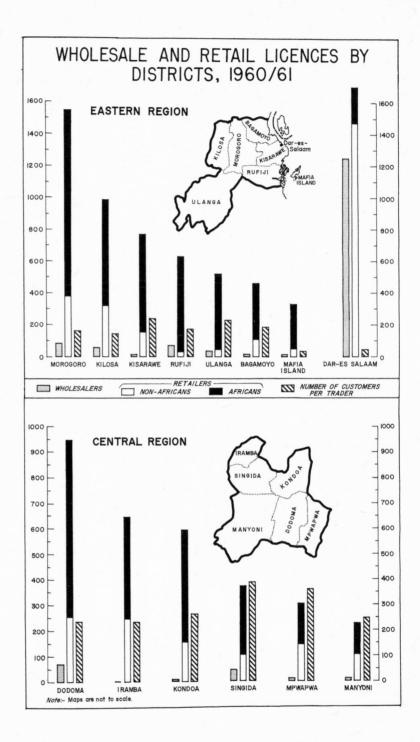

WHOLESALE AND RETAIL LICENCES BY
DISTRICTS, 1960/61

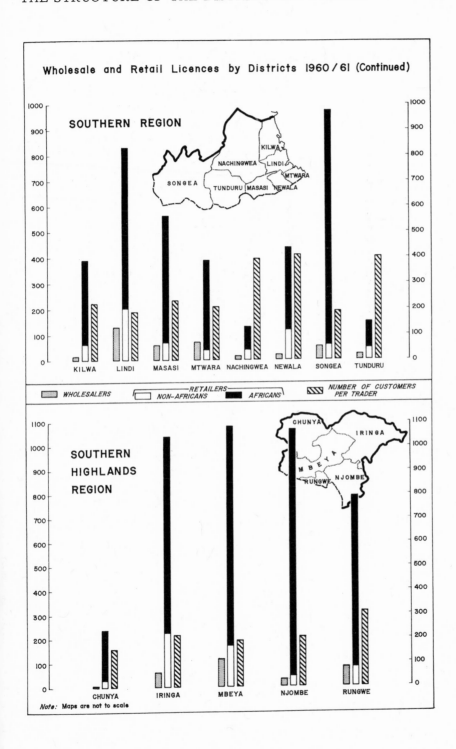

Wholesale and Retail Licences by Districts 1960/61 (Continued)

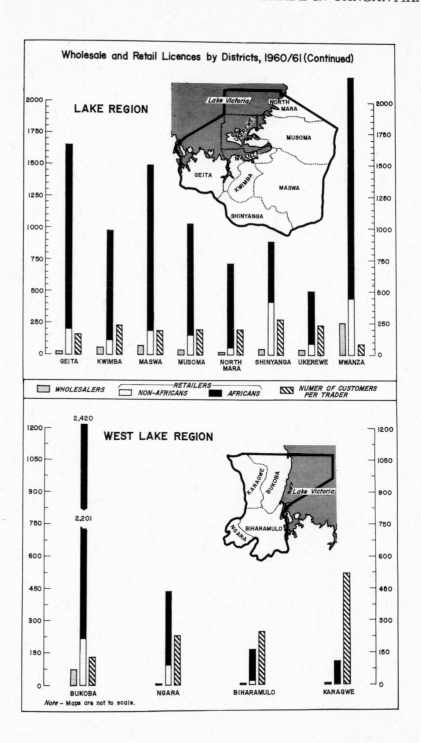

Wholesale and Retail Licences by Districts, 1960/61 (Continued)

LAKE REGION

WEST LAKE REGION

WHOLESALERS   RETAILERS NON-AFRICANS   AFRICANS   NUMER OF CUSTOMERS PER TRADER

Note - Maps are not to scale.

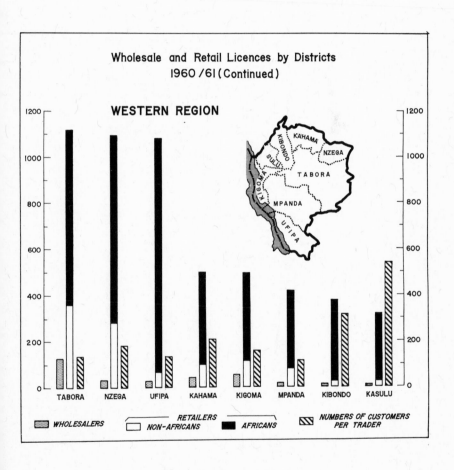

Wholesale and Retail Licences by Districts
1960 /61 (Continued)

WESTERN REGION

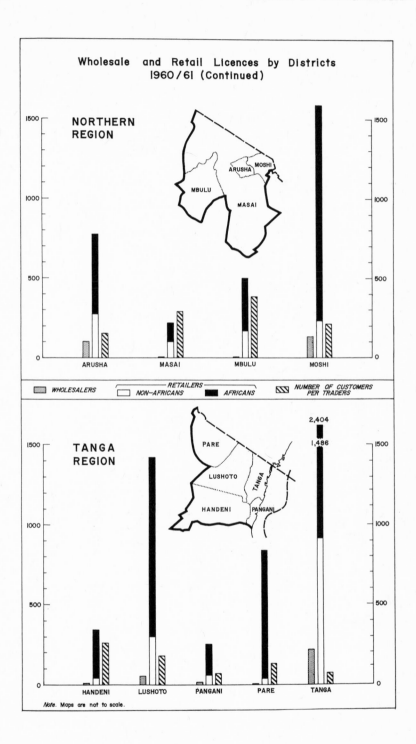

Wholesale and Retail Licences by Districts
1960/61 (Continued)

NORTHERN REGION

ARUSHA   MASAI   MBULU   MOSHI

WHOLESALERS   RETAILERS — NON-AFRICANS / AFRICANS   NUMBER OF CUSTOMERS PER TRADERS

TANGA REGION

2,404
1,486

HANDENI   LUSHOTO   PANGANI   PARE   TANGA

Note. Maps are not to scale.

other regions; finally, they produce more of the minor cash crops, which are not marketed by co-operatives, so that there is probably a large number of wholesalers who are mainly dealing in local produce. There is in fact a very high proportion of wholesalers in these two regions which is not licensed to export or import. These wholesalers are, by and large, the smaller ones in trading centres and minor settlements, who are wholesaling to African shopkeepers and buying local produce.

ESTIMATED POPULATION AND MONETARY INCOME BY REGIONS, 1961

Region	Population '000	Monetary Income	
		Total $ million	Per head $ million
Dar es Salaam	138	35.6	257.6
Eastern	1,020	34.4	33.6
Central	950	12.0	12.6
Southern Highlands	1,100	22.1	20.2
West Lake	550	8.1	14.8
Lake	1,855	64.7	34.7
Tanga	735	51.8	70.3
Western	1,140	24.1	21.3
Northern	825	35.6	43.1
Southern	1,085	29.7	27.4
Total	9,400	317.8	33.9

Note: The population estimates are based on the 1957 census adjusted by the estimated average annual rate of increase over the last four years. No account is taken of possible inter-regional migrations. The estimates of monetary income by regions are preliminary and should be used only as a rough guide to the relative positions of the regions.

Sources Estimates based on Tanganyika Statistical Abstract 1961 and Ministry of Finance.

The Eastern Region contains very few wholesalers who
either import or export, but a good many plain wholesalers,
and in particular branch wholesalers, mainly in Ulanga Dis -
trict and at Morogoro. The reason for the small number of
importers and exporters is of course that the wholesalers who
perform these functions for the Eastern Region are all found
in Dar es Salaam, figures for which are shown separately. Dar
es Salaam is the commercial centre of the Eastern Region,
with Morogoro and to a lesser extent Kilosa as subsidiary
wholesaling centres. These supply their respective districts,
in both of which there are good markets among sisal estate
workers and cash-crop farmers.

Dodoma is the commercial centre of the Central Region,
where the main wholesalers are located. Singida is also an
important subsidiary wholesaling centre. Part of its significance lies in its being in some sense an entrepot centre. It
lies midway on the only road connecting the Eastern half of
Tanganyika with the Lake Region. The road until this year has
not been an all-weather road, and crosses a very difficult,
swampy stretch just west of Singida. The traders in Singida
possess the local knowledge about conditions on this stretch
and, as a result, a great deal of the trade between these two
parts of Tanganyika has been in their hands. The wholesalers
in Singida fear that the opening of the new all-weather road
from Singida to Nzega in 1962 will damage their business. Undoubtedly the total traffic passing through Singida will be
greatly increased, but it will tend to be conducted by merchants
at either end of the route, i.e. in Mwanza or Moshi. With the
opening of an all-weather road, the local knowledge of road
conditions held by the Singida traders will no longer be of any
importance. Furthermore, with the very poor conditions
which used to prevail on the Singida-Nzega stretch, risks were
great and the profits correspondingly higher. These will now
be reduced. Smaller subsidiary wholesaling centres in the
Central Province are Mpwapwa and Gulwe, Kondoa, and
Manyoni.

Mbeya is the largest commercial centre in the Southern
Highlands Region, containing 99 of the region's 286 wholesalers.
But the region is slightly unusual in having three commercial
centres; Mbeya, Iringa and Tukuyu, all of almost equal importance. There is no one main central distributing point, as for
instance, Dodoma tends to be in the Central Region. There is
no railway line in the Southern Highlands. Goods are brought
by road into the region and are delivered direct to the wholesaler in Mbeya, Iringa or Tukuyu. Njombe is a subsidiary

wholesaling centre, to which most of the goods are delivered direct, but some pass through the traders in Iringa.

In the Western Region Tabora is the commercial centre. But as the region covers such a vast area, almost equal to that of the United Kingdom, the subsidiary wholesaling centres assume a considerable importance. The largest is Kigoma. Other important centres are Kahama, Mpanda and Sumbawanga.

Mwanza is by far the largest and most important commercial centre in the Lake Region;   there are more wholesalers there than in Tanga, though their total turnover is probably less. But Mwanza does not hold an unchallenged position as the distribution centre of the Lake Region. As we have seen there are more wholesalers in the Lake Region than in any other region, but less than half of them are in Mwanza itself. In no other region are there so many wholesalers in all the various districts of the region, and these wholesalers are not merely sub-wholesalers selling in small quantities to African shops. Many are in a substantial way of business. For instance, in all the districts except Geita there are at least a dozen wholesalers who are also licensed to import from abroad. Outside Mwanza there are the important wholesaling centres of Musoma and Shinyanga, and lesser centres such as Tarime, Maswa, Nansio, Ngudu, Malampaka and others.

There are various reasons for this large number of wholesalers in the region outside Mwanza. The region is the richest and most densely populated in Tanganyika. This naturally encourages the growth of townships and trading centres. Mwanza is also at the meeting point and terminus of two lines of communication, one across the lake from Kisumu and Mombasa and the other up the railway line from Dar es Salaam. Musoma receives direct shipments of goods from Kisumu and Mombasa by lake steamer, while Shinyanga obtains its supplies direct by rail from Dar es Salaam. Both are independent of Mwanza. Tarime can be most cheaply supplied from Musoma or across the border from Kenya. Likewise traders in a township on or near the railway line order direct from Dar es Salaam all goods which they can turnover in sufficient quantity. Only Geita District has to obtain practically speaking all its supplies from Mwanza, because of the lines of communication. Other districts obtain a large part of their requirements through Mwanza, but by no means all.

The commercial activity of the West Lake Region is very much concentrated in Bukoba. 72 out of the region's 87 wholesalers are located there. Ngara, Bugene and Biharamulo are the only other small centres of any importance. The population and purchasing power of the region are heavily concentrated in

the Bukoba area, so that this one centre can capture most of
the trade.

In the Tanga Region the distribution system is centred
largely on Tanga itself. Other subsidiary wholesaling centres
of importance are Korogwe and Lushoto, though Pangani and
Handeni are also minor centres of wholesaling. As in West
Lake, the population and particularly the purchasing power are
concentrated in a fairly small area, easily accessible by rail
and road, so that the business of wholesaling can likewise be
concentrated.

In the Northern Region the twin towns of Moshi and Arusha
dominate the commercial scene. All but 10 of the region's 249
wholesalers are in these two towns. Moshi supplies the densely
populated area round Mt. Kilimanjaro and Pare District, while
Arusha supplies its own district together with Masai and Mbulu.
Arusha has the smaller local trade, but it is something of a
centre for the produce trade of East Africa, being the head -
quarters of a big maize-growing region, while at the same
time it is very centrally placed between Kenya and Tanganyika,
and at the cross-road of two main routes, the Great North Road
and the east-west route connecting Mombasa, Tanga and Moshi
in the east with the Lake Region in the west.

In the Southern Region commerce is centred on the ports of
Lindi and Mtwara. These are in many ways an ill-matched
pair, since they merely duplicate each other's functions. Lindi
is the old-established port and commercial centre of the region.
Mtwara has a magnificent port created at great expense to serve
the ill-fated groundnut scheme. Official policy has on the whole
been to encourage the growth of Mtwara at the expense of Lindi.
Even so, Mtwara lags a long way behind Lindi as a commercial
centre. Its only real asset, now that the railway has been
closed, is the existence of its two deep-water berths. Lindi
is a lighterage port with a good anchorage for four ocean-going
vessels. However, in 1962 the port was closed to all ocean-
going traffic, which is now diverted to Mtwara.

Of the 399 wholesalers in the Southern Region, 128 are in
Lindi and 74 in Mtwara, i.e. just over half. Being a very large
region, there are several important subsidiary wholesaling
centres. The most important of these is Songea at the western
end of the region; others are Masasi, Newala, Tunduru and
to a lesser extent Nachingwea and Kilwa Kivinje.

One of the most remarkable features about the wholesalers
in the Southern Region is the very large number which are
licensed as subsidiary places of business, i.e. branches. There
are 165 branch wholesalers out of the total of 399 wholesalers

in the region. Almost a third of all the wholesalers in Tanganyika licensed as being a subsidiary place of business are in the
Southern Region. There seem to be various reasons for this.
Since Lindi and Mtwara duplicate each other, wholesalers tend
to have their head office in one and a branch in the other.
There are 72 wholesale branches licensed in these two townships. Some of these are branches with their head offices in
Dar es Salaam, since most supplies arrive at Lindi and Mtwara
via Dar es Salaam, but most of them are locally based firms
compelled to have two offices in order to cover both ports.

There are also a great many branch wholesalers licensed in
Songea, Masasi and Tunduru. Some of these are branches of
firms based in Lindi or Mtwara, but most are small branches
of local wholesalers. The local wholesaler has his business in
the township, with one or more branches in the trading centres
or minor settlements round. This is a system which used to be
common in other regions, but seems now to have almost disappeared except in the Southern Region. The main object of the
system was to set up a network of branches which could buy
local produce from the growers. In the other regions the marketing of the major cash crops has been carried out by co-
operatives for some years now, and as a result the incentive
to maintain branches has disappeared; but up to 1962, the
marketing of the main cash crops in the Southern Region, cashew
and cassava, was in the hands of the traders, and the system of
branches has been maintained.

Commission agents or manufacturers' representatives are
almost all concentrated in Dar es Salaam, 48 out of the total of
59. There are two in each of the towns of Tanga, Mwanza,
Mbeya, Iringa and Moshi and one in Arusha. There are also,
of course, in these towns branches of firms or even independent
firms which combine being manufacturers' representatives for
some lines and wholesalers for other lines. These firms have
wholesalers licences. All the licensed brokers are to be found
in Dar es Salaam except one in Tanga and one in Mwanza.

Non-African retailers

The non-African retailers who are also licensed to import
direct from abroad cater mostly for the European market. They
prefer to import direct certain foodstuffs, medicines, cosmetics and items of clothing, very often by post. They are thus
able to by-pass the wholesalers and keep a higher margin for
themselves. These non-African retailers with a licence to import from abroad are found mostly in areas where there is a
sizable European population, together perhaps with a fairly
wealthy Asian community. They are most numerous in Dar es

Salaam, Moshi, Arusha, Tanga, Musoma, Mwanza and Bukoba.
Other places where they are fairly numerous are Shinyanga,
Iringa, Mbeya, Oldeani in Mbulu District, Lushoto, Singida and
North Mara District. All these are centres of European popu -
lation except the last two. In the first list Musoma and Bukoba
seem to be rather out of place also, since they have compara -
tively small European populations. Singida is difficult to explai
but Musoma, Bukoba and North Mara District are all near the
border with Kenya or Uganda. Though it is not necessary to ha
a licence to import, either as a retailer or wholesaler, if the
imports are merely from the other East African territories,
there is considerable confusion on this point among traders, wh
came to light during this enquiry. Many of these retailers li -
censed to import are only importing from Kenya or Uganda. Th
same is probably true of some of the large number of wholesale
licensed to import in Mwanza, Moshi and Arusha, as well as
Bukoba and Musoma.

    As we have seen already, non -African produce buyers are
really retailers with a licence also to buy produce from African
growers, and should be treated as retailers together with those
licensed purely to retail.

    The total number of non -African retailers licensed in 1961
was 10, 090. This compares with 3, 864 wholesalers. There
were therefore two and a half times as many non -African retail
ers as wholesalers. On the other hand, as there is no sharp
distinction between wholesalers and retailers, many of the tra -
ders doing a little wholesaling in addition to their retailing have
a much smaller turnover than some of the bigger retailers who
do no wholesaling. Almost all the Arab traders, whom we estimate number about 2, 500, are in the category of non -African
retailers. Many of their shops are very small indeed. It shoul
not be thought that the Asian retailers are all necessarily larger
than either the African or the Arab. Most probably are, but
there are many hundreds, even perhaps thousands, who have a
very small turnover indeed.

    The Lake Region, with 1, 643 licensed in 1961, had the larges
number of non -African retailers, followed by Dar es Salaam
with 1, 475. Tanga Region was third with 1, 365, a very large
number in relation to the population of the region. Eastern
Region was fourth, Western fifth, Central sixth, all with over
1, 000, then there is a sharp drop to the Northern Region with
800 and Southern with 647. Southern Highlands had 615 and,
finally, West Lake, a long way behind, with only 334.

    Where there is an unusually large number of non -African
retailers, it is generally because the number of Arab retailers

is particularly high. Since 74 per cent of gainfully occupied
Arabs were employed in the wholesale and retail trade at the
time of the 1957 census, the distribution of the Arab popula -
tion gives a fairly clear indication of the distribution of Arab
retailers. The Arab population was heavily concentrated in
certain areas. In Tanga Region there were 4, 037 Arabs,
mainly in Tanga District, in Western Region 3, 101, mainly
in Nzega and Tabora Districts, in Lake Region 3, 073, mainly
in Shinyanga District. There were 2, 545 Arabs in Dar es
Salaam, 2, 659 in Eastern Region, spread throughout the re -
gion except in Ulanga District, 1, 764 in Central Region, being
most numerous in Dodoma and Iramba Districts. There were
less than 300 Arabs in the Northern, Southern and Southern
Highlands Regions.

The distribution of the Arab traders in the various districts
seems to be decided as much by historical factors and custom
as by economic considerations. They are most numerous along
the northern half of the coast, particularly in Tanga and Dar
es Salaam. Their other main area of concentration is in the
four adjoining districts of Tabora, Nzega, Shinyanga and Iram -
ba. Tabora was originally an important Arab trading centre
on the old slave route from the coast to Lake Tanganyika, and
undoubtedly formed the nucleus of this settlement. The fairly
large number of Arabs distributed through Eastern and Central
Regions is also largely a relic of this old slave trading route.

This examination of the distribution of Arab traders is in a
sense a digression, but it helps to explain some of the apparent
anomalies in the distribution of non-African retailers. On the
regional level the distribution of Arab retailers seems mainly
to increase the density of non-African retailers where these
are already thick on the ground. Even when the Arab retailers
have been discounted, the other non-African retailers, i. e.
the Asians, are still most numerous in the same selection of
regions. The most striking feature of the distribution of Asian
retailers, after discounting the Arabs, is their extreme paucity
in the West Lake Region. There are probably less than 200
Asian retailers in the whole region.

Asian retailers are most numerous in the Lake, Tanga and
Eastern Regions. These regions, as we have noticed already,
combine between them large populations and high average mone -
tary incomes. The regions which have the smallest number of
Asian retailers, besides West Lake, are Southern Highlands,
Southern, Northern and Western Regions. West Lake Region
has a small population, only 550, 000, and Northern Region has
only 825, 000, but the other three regions all have around the

1,100,000 mark. All these regions, with the notable exception
of the Northern Region, have low average monetary incomes,
and this certainly accounts for the small number of Asian retailers in them. However, the Northern Region stands out as
an exception here, with an average monetary income well above
the rest. The reason for the lack of Asian retailers in the
region is that there are scarcely any outside the township of
Moshi in the densely populated and wealthy Moshi District. A
deliberate policy by the people of the Chagga tribe of forcing
the Asian traders out of the rural areas has been extremely
effective.

Central Region is rather a special case as far as the number
of non-African retailers is concerned. It is the poorest region
with a comparatively small population, yet it contains a relatively large number of non-African retailers. Many of these
are Arabs, but many also are Asians. The explanation for
this seems to be that there are very few African retailers,
fewer than in any other region, and their shops are usually
smaller than elsewhere. The local people have in fact only
recently shown any interest in retailing, and as yet little apti-
tude. The trade is still more in the hands of Asians and Arabs
than in other regions. Furthermore, there are hardly any
produce marketing co-operatives in the Central Region. The
buying of local produce is almost entirely in the hands of non-
African traders. Well over half the non-African retailers are
licensed to buy produce, a higher proportion than in any other
region except the Western Region.

Regions with a large number of licensed produce buyers
are Lake, Western, Eastern, Central and Southern. In the
last four of these, produce buyers form a high proportion of
total non-African retailers. In these regions marketing co-
operatives are little developed and a wide variety of minor
cash crops is grown. There are relatively few produce
buyers in West Lake and Tanga Regions. In West Lake very
little produce is marketed other than the coffee crop handled
by the co-operatives. In Tanga Region the main crops produced are the estate-grown crops of sisal and tea. The next
most important crop, copra, is handled by quite a small number of dealers.

Separate returns are made by town councils for non-
African retailers licensed to trade in the main townships.
These give a clear idea of the degree of urbanisation of non-
African retailers.

NON-AFRICAN RETAILERS LICENSED
BY TOWN COUNCILS, 1960-61

Dar es Salaam	1, 246
Tanga	503
Mwanza	241
Morogoro	172
Tabora	155
Dodoma	146
Moshi	140
Iringa	132
Arusha	105
Lindi	95
Mbeya	68
Bukoba	23
Total	3, 026

Source   Ministry of Finance.

Just under a third of all non-African retailers were located
in the twelve largest townships, and over half of these were in
Dar es Salaam and Tanga.   But it must be remembered that in
1957 these towns contained well over half of the population living in the twelve towns listed, 167, 000 out of a total of 286, 000,
so the proportion of non-African retailers in them is not unduly
high.
While there were 3, 026 non-African retailers in the twelve
largest towns, there were 7, 028 outside them in the rural areas,
minor settlements, trading centres and smaller townships. This
gives an average of 128 for each of Tanganyika's fifty-five districts and indicates a fairly wide dispersal throughout the country.   Clearly non-African retailers are more numerous in some
districts than others.   Districts with particularly few are Karagwe with only 4, Biharamulo with 18, both in the West Lake Region,
Chunya in the Southern Highlands with 27 and Kasulu and Kibondo
in the Western Region with 27 and 29 respectively.   But only in
seven other districts are there fewer than 50 non-African retailers.   There are in fact very few parts of the country with a

sizable population in which there is no non-African retailer. It
is only in the remote and thinly populated parts of Western and
Southern Regions that few or no Asian or Arab retailers are to
be found.

African retailers

There were 34,581 African retailers licensed in Tanganyika
in 1961. By far the largest number was to be found in the Lake
Region, 7,820 or between a quarter and a fifth of the total.
Second came the Western Region with 4,322, then Eastern Regi
with 4,157 and Tanga with 3,893. Central Region had the small
number, other than Dar es Salaam, with only 2,088. There we
only 2,396 in the Northern Region, though this figure is open to
some doubt as it shows a drop of 672 from the previous year an
probably reflects incomplete returns from Moshi District.

As has been pointed out already, African retailing seems to
be less developed in Central Region than in any other Region.
The Northern Region is made up of two sharply contrasted area
on the one hand the Moshi and Arusha Districts with dense and
comparatively wealthy populations, a great many African shops
and probably the most highly developed African retailing systen
in Tanganyika; on the other hand, the Districts of Masai and
Mbulu, sparsely populated, far from wealthy, with very few
African retailers indeed. In West Lake Region there is a similar contrast between Bukoba District and the Districts of Karag
we and Biharamulo; Ngara District comes somewhere in betwe

The distribution of African retailers by districts can be seer
most clearly from the charts pages 38-42. The contrast betwe
the number of African retailers in the Moshi and Arusha Dis -
tricts and the Masai and Mbulu Districts comes out clearly; als
the contrast in West Lake Region. In the Eastern Region there
is a heavy concentration of African traders in Morogoro Distric
while in Dar es Salaam, especially in comparison with the num
ber of non-African retailers, there are remarkably few. In the
Central Region there are very few African traders in the Distri
of Mpwapwa and Manyoni. In the Lake Region, Mwanza, Geita,
and Maswa Districts have relatively vast numbers of African re
tailers. Only Shinyanga and Ukerewe Districts have rather few
Shinyanga District has a particularly large number of non-Afric
traders, mostly Arabs, and Ukerewe District is rather sparsel
populated. In Southern Region, only in the large and fairly popu
lous district of Songea is there any considerable number of Afri
retailers. The Districts of Nachingwea and Tunduru have parti
cularly few, though it must be remembered that both are very
sparsely populated.

The figures for the Southern Highlands Region are somewhat

suspect, insofar as the number of African retailers licensed
in the Rungwe District fell from 1,501 in 1959-1960 to only
710 in 1960-61. Otherwise Njombe District has a fairly
large number of African retailers and Chunya District very
few, but its population is very small.

Tanga Region also presents some contrasts. Tanga and
Lushoto Districts being both populous and wealthy have a
great many African retailers. Pare District has a considerable number, though it is less populous and less wealthy. On
the other hand, as we have seen, there are extremely few non-
African retailers in the district. Pangani District appears to
have particularly few African retailers, but its population was
only 20,000 in 1957. Handeni District, with more African
traders than Pangani, is very much larger and with a much
larger population.

In Western Region there are a great many African retailers
in Ufipa District, and also in Nzega and Tabora Districts.
In Kasulu and Mpanda Districts on the other hand there are
relatively few, though Mpanda District is extremely sparsely
populated.

As with the non-African retailers, returns are made by
the twelve town councils of the number of African retailers
licensed, and thus some idea of the degree of urbanisation of
African traders can be obtained.

AFRICAN RETAILERS LICENSED
BY TOWN COUNCILS, 1960-61

Tanga	505
Mwanza	313
Dar es Salaam	230
Moshi	216
Morogoro	185
Dodoma	142
Tabora	83
Arusha	57
Lindi	51
Mbeya	50
Iringa	49
Bukoba	31
Total	1,912

Source Ministry of Finance

Unlike the Asian and Arab retailers, a very small proportio
of all African retailers is found in the twelve main towns,   only
just over 5 per cent. The overwhelming majority of African
shops is in rural areas.

The figure of 505 African retailers in Tanga township seems
surprisingly high and is almost certainly inflated by the practic
of Arab traders licensing their shops in the names of their Afri
wives, thus being able to obtain the cheaper African trader's l
cence. It seems probable that of all the towns, Mwanza may h;
the largest number of genuine African retailers within its boun
daries. There is also a comparatively large number in Moshi.
Considering its size there are very few African traders in Dar
es Salaam, where competition from Arab and Asian retailers i;
undoubtedly very intense. It is notable that both Mwanza and
Moshi are in areas where African retailing is more highly deve
loped.

The figures in the table above confirm the impression obtair
while travelling round the country in the course of this enquiry
that African retailers are very poorly represented in the towns
Considering the proportion of the urban population which is Afr
can, and more particularly the volume of African purchasing
power in the towns, it is clear that there are disproportionatel
few African retailers in the urban areas. This problem is
examined in more detail in Chapter 5.

The number of traders in relation to population

In order to obtain a true picture of the distribution of trader
in Tanganyika, we need to relate the number of traders license
to the population in each district and region and also, if possil
to the purchasing power of that population. If we divide the pop
lation figure for the district by the number of traders in it, we
obtain a figure for the average number of customers per trade;
that district. These customers, of course, include men, wom
and children, a high proportion being small infants, so that the
term customer should not be taken too literally. A more seric
problem is that the last census was taken in 1957, and no more
recent figures for the population by districts are available.   W
are compelled, therefore, to divide the 1957 population figure
the 1960-61 figure for licensed traders. However, the object (
obtaining these figures of the average number of customers pe
trader is to be able to make comparisons between districts an
regions. This discrepancy between the dates of the population
of the licence figure introduces an element of unreliability, but
does not destroy the usefulness of the resultant average as a b;
for comparison. It must, however, be remembered that these
average figures provide only a very rough method of comparis(

POPULATION AND NUMBER OF CUSTOMERS PER TRADER,
NON-AFRICAN, AFRICAN AND ALL RACES

Region and District	Population 1957 '000	Customers per		
		Non-African trader	African trader	Trader of all races
Dar es Salaam	129	47	5,610	44
Eastern Region	956	693	230	173
Bagamoyo	89	695	254	186
Kilosa	153	405	230	146
Kisarawe	188	1,130	305	240
Mafia	12	200	43	35
Morogoro	267	575	228	164
Rufiji	119	1,180	198	170
Ulanga	127	1,550	268	229
Central Region	887	766	425	273
Dodoma	240	740	347	236
Kondoa	159	970	362	264
Manyoni	59	500	480	245
Mpwapwa	116	755	705	363
Singida	163	1,085	605	389
Iramba	151	610	380	233
Southern Highlands Region	1,030	1,143	280[a]	230[a]
Chunya	38	1,225	182	158
Iringa	249	715	306	214
Mbeya	231	805	253	193
Njombe	241	3,350	234	220
Rungwe	271	1,665	380[a]	310[a]
West Lake Region	514	1,221	184	160
Bukoba	308	1,060	140	124
Karagwe	63	5,730	575	520
Biharamulo	41	1,865	283	248
Ngara	102	1,050	300	232

POPULATION AND NUMBER OF CUSTOMERS PER TRADER,
NON-AFRICAN, AFRICAN AND ALL RACES (Continued).

Region and District	Population 1957 '000	Customers per		
		Non-African trader	African trader	Trader all rac
Lake Region	1,732	790	222	173
Geita	270	1,200	186	161
Kwimba	242	1,450	280	235
Maswa	292	1,120	224	187
Mwanza	197	285	112	80
Musoma	202	1,075	230	189
North Mara	145	1,835	220	195
Shinyanga	256	560	530	272
Ukerewe	127	1,040	305	236
Tanga Region	688	412	177	124
Handeni	90	1,690	310	261
Lushoto	269	750	240	182
Pangani	20	267	106	76
Pare	109	2,475	136	129
Tanga	200	176	135	76
Western Region	1,063	756	246	186
Kahama	113	785	234	209
Kasulu	175	4,725	610	540
Kibondo	120	3,640	345	315
Kigoma	87	495	233	158
Mpanda	50	480	151	115
Nzega	205	650	252	182
Tabora	167	342	222	135
Ufipa	145	1,450	142	130
Northern Region	772	735	322[b]	224[b]
Arusha	149	385	250	152
Masai	65	620	550	291
Mbulu	194	1,085	595	385
Moshi	365	1,050	269[b]	211[b]

POPULATION AND NUMBER OF CUSTOMERS PER TRADER,
NON-AFRICAN, AFRICAN AND ALL RACES (Continued).

Region and District	Population 1957 '000	Customers per		
		Non-African trader	African trader	Trader of all races
Southern Region	1,014	974	319	240
Kilwa	89	1,155	270	219
Lindi	178	540	286	187
Masasi	151	1,125	307	242
Mtwara	96	835	277	208
Nachingwea	56	950	667	392
Newala	177	1,250	557	385
Songea	197	1,670	216	191
Tunduru	70	970	690	402
Tanganyika	8,786	635	254	181

a.   The return for African traders in Rungwe District shows
a sharp fall from the figure for the previous year and is probably incomplete, thus affecting the ratios given here for Rungwe
and the Southern Highlands Region.

b.   The return for African traders in Moshi District appears
likewise to be incomplete.

Sources   Tanganyika Statistical Abstract 1961 and Ministry of
Finance.

The table and charts show how traders are distributed throughout the districts of Tanganyika in relation to the population of those
districts. Another important factor affecting the distribution of
traders is the volume of purchasing power in each district. Unfortunately the only figures available are of gross monetary income
by regions, not by districts. These figures are given in the table
on page 43. However, they do provide a useful guide to the volume
of purchasing power in different areas.

If we divide the estimated monetary income of each region
by the number of traders in that region, we obtain a figure
which shows the estimated monetary income of the population
of that region per trader there. This figure is <u>not</u> the average
income per trader. It is merely an average figure of the mone
tary income of the populations of the various regions in rela -
tion to the number of traders. If the figure is high, this indi -
cates that there are few traders in the region in relation to the
purchasing power available there. If the figure is low, it indicates that there are many traders in relation to the purchasing
power available.

THE ESTIMATED MONETARY INCOME
OF EACH REGION DIVIDED BY THE NUMBER
OF TRADERS, AFRICAN AND NON-AFRICAN

Region	Per non-African trader $	Per African trader $	Per trader of all races $
Dar es Salaam	12, 880	-	12, 068
Eastern	24, 836	8, 232	6, 188
Central	10, 276	5, 712	3, 668
Southern Highlands	24, 640	6, 048	4, 956
West Lake	19, 460	2, 940	2, 548
Lake	29, 400	8, 288	6, 440
Tanga	33, 040	13, 328	9, 044
Western	17, 136	5, 572	4, 200
Northern	33, 936	14, 868	10, 332
Southern	28, 700	9, 380	7, 056
Tanganyika	22, 960	9, 184	6, 552

<u>Source</u>   Estimates based on Ministry of Finance figures.

There is approximately one trader in Tanganyika to every
181 people. Both wholesale and retail traders are included
in this calculation, but as almost all wholesalers also sell
retail, this in effect means that there is approximately one

retail outlet to every 180 people. The equivalent figure in the
United Kingdom in 1950 was one shop to every 74 people. Thus
in Tanganyika there are almost two and a half   times as many
potential customers to each shop as in the United Kingdom. But
when we remember that the national income per head in the
United Kingdom is roughly thirty-two times more than the monetary income per head in Tanganyika, it is clear that the average
turnover of Tanganyika's shops must be less than a tenth that of
shops in the United Kingdom.

The number of customers per trader of all races varies considerably from region to region. Dar es Salaam, with only 44
customers per trader, has very much the lowest number, but
its population also has by far the highest average monetary income, $258, against the national average of $33.9. In fact, in
spite of having more shops in relation to the population than any
other region in the country, the total monetary income of the
population per trader at $12,068 was still the highest for any
region, almost double the national average. This indicates that
the average turnover of shops in Dar es Salaam is higher than
elsewhere.

After Dar es Salaam there were fewer customers per trader
in Tanga Region than in any other region, 124 compared with
the national average of 181. But in this region also the average
income is high, $70.3, so that the total monetary income of the
population per trader of $9,044 was well above the average, only
exceeded by Dar es Salaam and possibly the Northern Region.
Again this indicates that the average turnover of traders in Tanga
Region is relatively high.

In the districts of Tanga and Pangani the number of customers
per trader is remarkably low, less than half the Tanganyika
average. There are a great many African and non-African traders in relation to the population. In both these districts there
are of course many sisal estate workers, so that the total cash
incomes earned are very high by Tanganyika standards.

A sharp contrast to Tanga Region is provided by the West
Lake Region. Here also there are comparatively few customers
per trader, only 160. However, the average income in the region is exceptionally low, at $14.8 per head it is the second
lowest of any region. Thus the total monetary income of the
population per trader is only $2,548, very much the lowest for
any region, and well under half the national average.   The
average turnover of traders in West Lake must be extremely
low, which indicates that there may be too many small shops.
The figures for the West Lake Region show that the excessive
number of traders is concentrated in the Bukoba District, where

there are only 124 customers per trader. In the other three
districts there are more customers per trader than the nationa
average, in Karagwe District considerably more. The figures
also show that it is the African traders in Bukoba District that
are so numerous. There are 1,060 customers per non-Africa
trader, well above the national average. For the whole region
there are 1,221 customers per non-African trader, almost
double the national average of 635. It does not seem, therefor
that it is the non-African traders that are too numerous in Wes
Lake Region. There is, in fact, a very heavy concentration of
African traders in the Bukoba District with a low average turnover.

With regard to the number of customers per trader, three
regions, Eastern, Lake and Western, are all clustered togethe
round the national average of 181. In both the Eastern and Lak
Regions, the total monetary incomes of the population per trader are very near the national average, but the figure $4,200
for Western Region is well below. The reason for this is that
in Eastern and Lake Regions the average monetary income is
more or less the same as for the country as a whole, while in
Western Region it is low, only $21.3 per head. Western Regio
therefore seems to have a rather large number of traders in
relation to the purchasing power of the people. The districts o
Kibondo and, to an even greater extent, Kasulu have many mor
customers per traders than the average. In other words there
is a considerable shortage of shops in relation to the size of th
population. However, the populations of these two districts ar
heavily concentrated in their north-western parts, and their
cash incomes are extremely low, so that it is doubtful whether
more shops could in fact be justified.

Most of the districts in the Eastern Region have about the
average number of customers per trader, but one district,
Mafia Island, stands out as having a quite exceptional number c
traders, both African and non-African. There is one shop to
every 35 persons on the island, which is approximately five
times the density of shops for Tanganyika as a whole. Kisaraw
and to a lesser extent Ulanga District have comparatively few
shops in relation to the population. No doubt the people of Kisa
rawe District tend to do much of their shopping in Dar es Salaa
Ulanga, Rufiji and Kasarawe Districts all have very few non-
African traders in relation to their population. In Ulanga this i
probably due to the extreme remoteness of much of the district
and the low level of cash incomes, as well as the complete ab -
sence of Arab traders.

In the Mwanza District in the Lake Region, there are very fe

customers per trader, only 80, less than half the national ave -
rage. This holds equally true for both African and non-African
traders in the district. In the Lake Region as a whole there are
comparatively few non-African traders in relation to the population. Only in the Mwanza and Shinyanga Districts is the number
of customers per non-African trader below the average. In
Shinyanga this is entirely due to the presence of a great many
Arabs. Since the region is a rich one, the reason for the number of non-African traders being slightly below average is pro -
bably to be found in the high density of the population; fewer
traders are needed in the rural areas to distribute effectively,
both wholesale and retail. The turnover of non-African traders
in the region is thus slightly above the national average.

The figures for the Southern Highlands Region are open to
some doubt because of the strong possibility that the return for
African traders in Rungwe District is incomplete. If the previous
year's licence figure is used, the number of customers per tra -
der in the Region is reduced from 230 to 194, not much above the
national average. Likewise the figure for Rungwe District in -
stead of being above the national average is reduced to a figure
slightly below it. In the region as a whole there appear to be
rather few non-African traders in relation to the population, but
the monetary income of the population per non-African trader is
only a little above the average. In other words in relation to
the income of the region, rather than its population, the number
of Asian and Arab traders is near the average for the country.
For African traders, however, this is not the case. Average
monetary income per trader is only $6,048 against the national
average of $9,184. The average turnover of African traders
in the Southern Highlands seems therefore to be low.

In the Northern Region we have the same problem of a sus -
pected incomplete return for African traders from Moshi Dis -
trict. Again if the previous year's licence figure is used, the
number of customers per trader comes down to just about the
national average, while for Moshi District it is well below the
national average. This is entirely due to the very large number of African traders licensed in that district in the previous
year. The number of Asian traders in relation to the population
of the district was well below the average.

Whether the 1960-61 licence figure or the higher one for the
previous year is used, the total monetary income of the region
per trader is high, per African trade and per non-African trader likewise. This is due to the high cash income per head of
the population of the region. It means that the average annual
turnover of both African and non-African traders is higher in

Northern than in other regions. This does not mean that among
the African shops in the Northern Region, there are not many
very small ones. There are, but there are also more rather
larger ones than in other regions. This applies to the Moshi
and Arusha Districts, not Masai and Mbulu. The contrast between the Moshi and Arusha Districts and most of the rest of
Tanganyika is masked to some extent because monetary income
figures are only available on a regional basis, and Northern
Region consists of the two wealthy districts of Moshi and Arusha
and the two poor districts of Masai and Mbulu. These last two
bring down the average for the region.

The districts of Masai and Mbulu both have a great many
customers per African trader, i.e. comparatively few African
traders in relation to the population, though almost certainly
not in relation to its monetary income. Mbulu District also
has few non-African traders, as shown by the high figure for
customers per non-African traders.

In the Southern Region the number of customers per non -
African trader, per African trader and per trader of any race
is in each case appreciably above the average. There are in
fact few traders of all races in relation to the population. This
is also true if taken in relation to the monetary income of the
region. It seems that there are comparatively few traders in
the Southern Region and their turnover is slightly higher than
the average.

Among the districts there is a considerable variation in the
number of customers per trader, though none has less than the
national average. Lindi and Songea have only just over the
average, but Tunduru, Nachingwea and Newala all have well
over double the national average, i.e. half as many traders as
the average in relation to the population. Tunduru and Nachingwea are sparsely populated and not wealthy, but in the case of
Newala the population density is the highest of any district in
the region and income from the sale of cash crops is considerab

The traders in Newala District undoubtedly have an average
turnover which is very much higher than that of the traders in
most other districts in Tanganyika. This is true of both the
African and Asian traders. There seem to be several reasons
for this. Newala in several ways is rather a special case.
For one thing, the wholesale trade and much of the produce trad
is dominated by one trader. This means that it is difficult for
new Asian traders to set up a business by obtaining goods on
credit from several competing wholesalers. The district is
densely populated with trading centres well distributed throughout. The Asian traders in these centres, obtaining their supplie

mainly from the one wholesaler, do much of the business therefore.   Another feature of Newala District is the remarkable
number of branch shops.   Probably over half of the African
shops in the district are in effect branches of Asian traders,
who supply them with all their goods.   This means that it is
difficult for an African trader to set up a new business.   There
are not many very small African shops in the district.   There
are fewer shops than the average but they are rather larger and
better stocked.

The situation in neighbouring Masasi District is to some extent similar, although there does not appear to be any one wholesaler in such a dominating position as in Newala District.   However, there seems to be the minimum of competition between
the various medium-sized wholesalers who are doing business
in Masasi.   They appear to act together to some extent to restrict the entrance of new Asian traders.   Again, as in Newala
District, a very large proportion of the African shops, probably
over half, are branches controlled by Asian traders.   64 of the
71 non-African retailers in the district are licensed to buy produce, as well as the 63 wholesalers.   Practically all these produce
buyers have at least one or two branches in the interior, managed by an African shopkeeper, whose main function is to buy
produce.   There are therefore rather few independent African
traders, especially in view of the density of the population over
much of the district and the comparatively high earnings of the
people from cash crops.

Finally we come to the Central Region, where the number
of customers per trader is well above the national average,
i.e.where there are few traders in relation to the population,
though not in relation to the monetary income.   The monetary
income of the population per trader is the lowest of any region
except West Lake.   Even though African traders are very thin
on the ground in relation to the population, the monetary income of the region per African trader is still very low,   well
below the national average.   Their average turnover is therefore also likely to be low.

There are slightly more customers per non-African trader
than the national average, in other words there are rather fewer
non-African traders than the average for Tanganyika.   Nevertheless, the monetary income of the region per non-African
trader is extremely low, by far the lowest of any region, and
only a little above the figure of the total monetary income of
Tanganyika per African trader.   As we have seen already, a
great many of the non-African traders in Central Region are
Arabs, and their turnover in many cases is very little, if at

all, higher than the turnover of many African traders.

The problem in the Central Region is that the level of cash incomes of the population as a whole is disastrously low, the lowest for any region in Tanganyika. The region produces a lower total value of cash crops than any other. None of the major cash crops is grown. There is very little paid employment in the region, again less than in any other. What little cash income is earned is obtained almost entirely from the sale of livestock and from a few minor cash crops. The result is that the purchasing power of the population is minimal and the volume of trade in the region very low indeed. What little trade there is, is mainly in the hands of Asian and Arab traders who themselves mostly have a very small turnover. African shops are comparatively few, and those that do exist are almost all very small. It does not seem on the whole that the large number of Arab retailers have up to now prevented the African retailers from increasing in number. It is rather that the Arab retailers have moved in to fill a vacuum, and without them the retailing facilities in the region would have been quite inade- quate. With cash incomes so low, it is very difficult for any of the local Africans to save enough money to open even the smallest of shops.

The situation in Central Region, with very low cash incomes and therefore very little trade and very few and inadequate shops, is by no means unusual in Tanganyika. The same state of affairs is to be found in Kasulu, Kibondo, Karagwe and Biha- ramulo Districts, as well as in large areas in other districts. Central Region is unique in that these conditions cover almost a whole region.

The ratio of wholesalers to retailers

Various new aspects of the structure of the distribution system are revealed by an examination of the ratio of whole- salers to retailers in each region, but these figures must be used with caution. As we have seen, there is no clear distinc- tion between the two categories, so that the ratio is in some ways deceptive. Under the category of wholesalers are grouped the large wholesalers who import and possibly export, the medium-sized wholesalers who do a mostly wholesaling busines but also a sizable retailing business, and finally the multitude of comparatively small traders, who do some wholesaling on a very small scale, almost entirely to African shops, but who als do a good deal of retail business. Under the category of retaile are included all those shops, Asian, Arab and African, which do a purely retail business, with no petty wholesaling, who have quite a large turnover, say of over $35,000 a year, but outside the main towns there are hardly any traders with a reasonably large turnover, say over $14,000 a year, who do not do some wholesaling.

From this it will be seen that the ratio of wholesalers to retailers is, in effect, the ratio of the fairly large traders to the rather small traders.

THE AVERAGE NUMBER OF RETAILERS
PER WHOLESALER BY REGIONS

Dar es Salaam	1.3
Eastern	20
Central	21
Southern Highlands	17
West Lake	36
Lake	17
Tanga	17
Western	16
Northern	16
Southern	10
Tanganyika	11

Source   Table on pages 34 and 35.

There are several rather striking features about this table. In five of the regions the ratio is remarkably similar, Southern Highlands, Lake, Tanga, Western and Northern. In Eastern and Central Regions the number of retailers per wholesaler is rather higher, 20 and 21. For the rest the ratio in the Southern Region is exceptionally high while in West Lake it is exceptionally low. Dar es Salaam is in a class by itself.

The five regions with a ratio of one to 16 or 17 do not seem to have any other features in common. This ratio seems to indicate the normal balance between large and small traders. In the Eastern Region, one would expect the number of retailers in relation to the number of wholesalers to be high, since most of the main wholesalers for the region are located in Dar es Salaam. In Central Region the large number of retailers per wholesaler reflects the high proportion of small shops in the region.

Conversely the small number of retailers per wholesaler in the
Southern Region reflects the high proportion of rather larger
shops which are found in that region. We have already remarked
that the average turnover of traders in the Southern Region is
fairly high, and that this is partly due to the prevalence of the
system of branch shops, the branches tending to be larger than
the large number of small independent African shops which
exist in other regions.

In Dar es Salaam there are 1,253 wholesalers to 1,705 retailers; while one would expect to find many wholesalers there,
since it is the commercial centre of the country, the very high
figure deserves closer examination. Dar es Salaam in this con-
text can be taken to fulfil two commercial functions. It is the
importing and primary wholesaling centre for all Tanganyika,
except for Tanga, Northern and West Lake Regions and about
half the Lake Region. It is also the secondary or local wholesaling centre for the Eastern Region and Dar es Salaam city
itself, though Morogoro is an important subsidiary centre in
the Region. If we take the Eastern Region and Dar es Salaam
together we might expect about 500 wholesalers to be engaged in
supplying the local trade. This is rather fewer than are licensed
in the Lake Region where the population is greater, but where
the total monetary income is about the same as in the Eastern
Region and Dar es Salaam combined. As there are 259 wholesalers in the Eastern Region, we might estimate that about 250
wholesalers in Dar es Salaam should be catering for the local
regional trade. This means that about 1,000 wholesalers are
left who supply the remaining four and a half regions, i.e. Cent:
Southern Highlands, Southern, Western and half Lake, as prima
wholesalers.

This division is of course unreal. There are not in fact 250
wholesalers in Dar es Salaam merely supplying the sub-wholesalers and retailers of the City and the Eastern Region while the
other 1,000 wholesalers supply the rest of the country. Nevertheless it does not seem unreasonable to assume that the City an
the Region provide trade which could be adequately conducted by
250 wholesalers. A more serious problem arises from the fact
that a great many of Dar es Salaam's 1,253 wholesalers are in
fact retailers who only do very occasional wholesaling. Without
carrying out a full-scale census of distribution, it is impossible
to say exactly how many fall into this category. There might at
a guess be about 400, though it seems unlikely that there are
more, since out of the total of 1,253 wholesalers, there are 781
licensed either to import or import and export.

If, therefore, we deduct 400 from the 1,000 wholesalers, we

are still left with 600 wholesalers in Dar es Salaam dealing
with the up-country trade. In the four and a half regions there
are 1,436 wholesalers, plus 95 retailers who are licensed to
import and who might be supposed to buy also direct from Dar
es Salaam. Very few traders up-country who have only a retail
licence buy their supplies direct from Dar es Salaam, though
there are some in the larger towns and trading centres who do.
On the other hand a great many of the traders up-country who
are licensed as wholesalers are only sub-wholesalers in small
trading centres and minor settlements. These sub-wholesalers
buy most, if not all, their supplies from a local wholesaler
within the region, and in the Southern Region, for instance,
very few of them, outside Lindi and Mtwara, deal direct with
Dar es Salaam. It seems, therefore, that there are at the outside about 1,500 wholesalers and retailers up-country in Central, Southern Highlands, Southern Western and Lake Regions
who are dealing direct with wholesalers in Dar es Salaam.

Thus there appear to be roughly 600 wholesalers in Dar es
Salaam supplying about 1,500 traders up-country. These figures are only very approximate, but they do indicate the order
of magnitude of the figures we are dealing with. There is in
fact something like one wholesaler in Dar es Salaam to every
two or three traders up-country who are dealing direct with
Dar es Salaam. This is an extraordinarily high ratio, and
suggests that many of the wholesalers in Dar es Salaam cannot
possibly be carrying out the full range of wholesaling functions.
It is perfectly clear in fact that the bulk of the trade is handled
by perhaps 100 to 150 large or fairly large firms, while the remainder are in a very small way of business indeed. The question of course arises whether there are not too many wholesalers in Dar es Salaam. This raises a great many issues, and
cannot really be dealt with until we have examined further aspects
of the distribution system.

Itinerant traders

Most itinerant traders are African, though there are also
many Arabs. A few Asian traders take out itinerant traders'
licences in order to be able to send trucks or pick-ups round the
local markets, etc.

Many of the itinerant traders licensed in certain regions are
cattle dealers. This is particularly the case in the Lake and
Central Regions, and to a lesser extent in the Northern and Southern Highlands Regions. Most itinerant traders, however, are
peddling piecegoods, fancy goods and a small selection of sundry
items. The hawker does not usually saddle himself with standard
goods, such as americani or kaniki, on which the margin is very

small. He normally carries dress materials, khangas perhaps,
shirts, beads, cheap jewellery and the like. He may have a
bicycle or travel on foot or by 'bus.

There were 11,576 itinerant traders' licences issued in Tanganyika in the 1960-61 licensing year. By far the largest number was in the Tanga Region, with a total of 3,112. Other
regions with over a thousand itinerant traders licensed were
West Lake, Northern, Lake and Western. There were very few
itinerant traders in the Southern and Central Regions and comparatively few in the Eastern and Southern Highlands Regions.

There were four districts with an outstandingly large number
of itinerant traders, Lushoto with 1,463, Bukoba with 1,042,
Tanga with 1,000 and Moshi with 728. All these districts are
rather densely populated, comparatively rich, with the possible
exception of Bukoba, and all have a particularly large number
of permanent retail shops. Other districts with many itinerant
traders were Arusha, Handeni, Morogoro, Nzega, Musoma,
Mbulu, Shinyanga, Karagwe, Njombe and Maswa; the traders
in these districts range in number from 411 in Arusha to 251 in
Maswa District. Half of these ten districts have a large number of regular traders also, i.e. Arusha, Morogoro, Nzega,
Maswa and Musoma. Njombe has many regular traders, almost
all African, but in relation to the large population of the district
they are not so numerous. Handeni and Shinyanga have rather
more customers per trader than the average i.e. comparatively
few regular traders. It is noticeable that both these districts
are bordered by other districts in which itinerant traders are
particularly numerous. Only Mbulu and Karagwe Districts of
these ten have really very few permanent traders in relation to
the size of their populations.

On the whole, itinerant traders tend to be most numerous in
the densely populated rich districts, where there is plenty of
trade and there are also plenty of regular shops. However, a
good many itinerant traders also operate in the more remote
districts where there are few regular shops. Of the sixteen
districts with the fewest traders in relation to the population,
there were ten with over one hundred licensed itinerant traders.
Of the six districts with few regular traders and also few itinerant traders, four were in the Southern Region and two in the
Central Region.

There were only 5 itinerant traders licensed in Masasi District, 13 in Tunduru and Nachingwea and 47 in Newala. In all
these districts it would seem to be desirable to encourage itinerant traders, but particularly in Tunduru and Nachingwea, districts with respectively the third and fourth lowest number of

regular traders in relation to population. It is worth noting that besides having so few itinerant traders, these districts also have the smallest absolute number of African traders of all the districts in Tanganyika.

In the Central Region, Manyoni and Mpwapwa Districts have very few itinerant traders as well as few regular traders, in particular Mpwapwa. Again it would seem to be desirable to encourage more itinerant traders. These two districts, after Tunduru, Nachingwea and Masai, have the next smallest absolute number of African traders of all the districts in the country. Masai District, incidentally, has a great many itinerant traders.

The licensing authority, i.e. the local administration in each district, has considerable powers to restrict itinerant traders; it may refuse to grant or at any time revoke a licence to engage in itinerant trading, or prescribe conditions upon which such a licence is issued. On the other hand, in no circumstances may a valid application for a wholesaler's or retailer's licence be refused.

In certain districts this right to refuse or restrict itinerant traders' licences is certainly used, and in many districts the established regular traders urge that the number of itinerant traders should be reduced by withholding licences. The itinerant trader undoubtedly provides additional competition for the established trader. The established trader tends to brand this competition as unfair, in that the itinerant trader supposedly has no overheads, while he, the established trader, has to pay for and maintain his shop premises, and in a town or trading centre he has to observe certain standards of hygiene and construction. In fact, the itinerant trader also has overheads, though of a different sort. He has considerable travelling expenses; even if he travels on foot, his time and subsistence cost something. He also suffers considerable risk of loss or damage to his goods through travel and the weather. The itinerant trader in Tanganyika is not normally accused of undermining standards of hygiene or health. He seldom deals in foodstuffs in any case. It is sometimes suggested, however, that the itinerant trader is more prone to cheat, exploit and indulge in barter and that, as he is constantly moving, he can get away with cheating his customers more easily. This last suggestion does perhaps have some truth in it, though customers are usually aware of this problem and are even more on their guard against fraud than when buying in an established shop. On the other hand, it would be extremely difficult to collect any very convincing evidence to show that the established shopkeeper's inability to move rapidly does anything to reduce his propensity to strike the most advantageous bargain, whether this is strictly honest or not.

In fact, itinerant trading is a perfectly legitimate form of trading and brings many advantages to the consumer. Frequently the goods are brought to the door, thus sparing the customer the need to travel to the nearest shop or trading centre. In rural areas the presence of hawkers with their wares at local markets greatly increases the range of goods on sale in that area, and helps considerably to expand the cash economy. In towns and trading centres the advantages are less obvious. However, the African customer, who may make very few purchases from a trader of any sort in the course of a year, prefers to do his shopping in a familiar open market, with the goods laid out on the ground for him to see. Instead of going into a shop and having to ask an often grudging shopkeeper to bring down goods off his shelves, the shopper can wander among the display of goods laid out by the hawkers and see exactly what is available. He feels much more at ease. When walking into a shop he imme-diately feels at a disadvantage with respect to the shopkeeper on the other side of the counter, while in the market he feels able to deal on more or less equal terms.

For an established trader, whether he be African, Asian or Arab, it is very galling to see itinerant traders selling their wares, often just in front of his shop, taking he feels, his busi-ness from him. His normal reaction is to demand that itinerant traders be banned, though as we have seen this would not benefit the consumer. Another reaction could be to improve the display and if necessary the prices in his shop, and perhaps to improve his approach to his customers.

The trader who is hardest hit by the activities of the hawkers is undoubtedly the small African shopkeeper who is trying to ex-tend the very limited range of his stock and build up his business by ploughing back his profits. The hawker has a fairly small stock of what, for the small established trader, are slow-moving lines, and which show rather higher profit margins. The hawker is able to turn over his small stock rather more quickly than the shopkeeper by travelling round to many different markets in fairl quick succession. He thus tends to skim off the cream of the bus ness, leaving the small local shopkeeper with the fast-moving bul lines, on which there is a much smaller margin. However, mos of the business in rural areas is in these lines, such as sugar, kerosene, flour, kaniki and americani, so that the activities of the hawkers do not seriously reduce the shopkeeper's turnover; but they do make it difficult for him to branch out beyond this li-mited trade, to build up his stock of the more slow-moving lines, to improve the scope and appearance of his shop, and thus attrac customers from rather further afield to come and make more than just their routine purchases.

If the question of restricting the number of itinerant traders' licences is raised, it should be remembered that this can practically never benefit the consumer, and is usually likely to inconvenience him quite seriously. The only valid reason for restricting hawkers' licences is in order to try and help build up the small shopkeeper. However, the existence of hawkers is only one of the difficulties facing the small shopkeeper, and not often a very serious one. It should also be remembered that both the small shopkeeper and the hawker are usually Africans. The hawker may be building up a thriving business in just the same way as the shopkeeper. There seems to be no valid reason for preventing him from doing this.

The hawker usually suffers from two rather serious disabilities. A good deal more prestige generally attaches to the ownership of a shop. The shopkeeper often has considerable influence in his own community, and can therefore mobilise local opinion against hawkers. Further, the authorities tend to have an uneasy suspicion that they cannot control and supervise the activities of a hawker, and therefore that he is in some way undesirable. Again it would be extremely difficult to show that the authorities have any greater control over the activities of an established shopkeeper than over those of a hawker. These factors should not be allowed to obscure the services to the consumer provided by the hawker, especially in rural areas. In general it seems clear that hawkers should not be restricted, and that in certain areas they should be actively encouraged.

THE CHANNELS OF DISTRIBUTION

Channels of distribution for different types of goods can take many forms; this is as true for the distributive system of Tanganyika as for anywhere else. Goods can be distributed by the manufacturer himself, by his representatives through various systems of exclusive agencies, authorised dealers, or tied outlets; they can be distributed through wholesalers or direct to retailers by van, or by a combination of the two. An enormous variety of arrangements can be made about the financing of stocks, methods of payment etc. The goods can be distributed in several forms, and various stages of food-processing, bulk-breaking and repacking can be undertaken at different levels in the distribution system. All these factors and many others combine to make the distribution network an extremely complex subject for analysis.

This survey is designed to cover the whole distribution system of Tanganyika. The channels of distribution of the products
of one industry alone could well form the subject of a complete
study if examined in full detail. It is only possible here to give
a very general picture of the various channels at present most
commonly used to distribute the main categories of goods.

There are three principal factors which govern the type of
distribution channel used in any set of circumstances: the
characteristics of the product to be distributed, the charac -
teristics of the market in which it is to be sold and, finally, the
availability of distributive resources. All three have influenced
the formation of the channels of distribution in Tanganyika.

It is usual to portray channels of distribution schematically
by means of flow charts, and it would be possible to prepare a
series of such diagrams for Tanganyika's trade. However,
they would be of doubtful value, and more likely to mislead than
to assist. Such charts give an impression of clearly defined
distributive functions and stages, and suggest a stability of trading relationships that is absent in Tanganyika. As a result of
the lack of specialisation, either by stages of distribution or by
types of trade, the same firm, on the same premises, normally
transacts business in many lines of goods in units of widely
different size. In general, all those engaged in one stage of
distribution are also likely to participate in most, if not all,
subsequent stages. It would not be possible to chart this state
of affairs satisfactorily.

In general, the channels of distribution in Tanganyika have
taken shape somewhat haphazardly in accordance with local requirements and circumstances. There has been very little conscious moulding of them by manufacturers or traders. In
Western Europe or America the process of organising a distribution network according to the requirements of his products is
often undertaken by the manufacturer. However, there are very
few large-scale manufacturers in East Africa, and only two
have organised a comprehensive distribution system of their
own. Occasionally large-scale retailers or wholesalers carve
out their own channels of distribution, but this has not happened
in Tanganyika. The whole network is made up of thousands of
individual distributors, each obtaining his supplies from the
sources most convenient for himself according to his particular
circumstances. There are no chain stores or multiples in Tanganyika. Scarcely any distributors have more than two or at the
most three branches primarily concerned with distribution
rather than produce-buying.

Moreover, goods are not forced through the distribution system under much pressure. There is very little active sales
promotion and little attempt by manufacturers or distributors to
push their wares. A chart of the channels of distribution would
show the goods being poured in at the top of the system by importers and local producers; they then trickle down through the
system, and at each junction point where there is a distributor
some goods pass on down the system while others flow out into
the hands of the consumers. The goods which percolate right
down through the system will be distributed in a fine spray
through the 45, 000 or so retailers and 11, 500 itinerant traders
who form the ultimate outlets of the distribution system.   But
not all of the goods complete the journey from top to bottom of
the system;   many leak out into the hands of the consumers at
all stages on the way down. This is, of course, only another
way of saying that almost all the wholesalers also sell retail.
It is also a way of indicating that a large part of the goods bought
by consumers are bought from outlets which are not purely retailers but combine both wholesaling and retailing.

The suggestion that the goods trickle down through the system
and are not pumped through it under pressure indicates that
distributors, with a few and occasionally notable exceptions, normally wait for a customer, either sub-wholesaler, retailer or
consumer, to come and make a purchase. There is very little
active selling or promotion of the vast bulk of consumer goods.

Piecegoods and clothing

The most typical of the consumer goods distributed in Tanganyika are piecegoods. They form by far the largest single
category of imported consumer goods, and for this reason it
seems appropriate to consider first how they are distributed.
The role of importers and wholesalers. Almost all piecegoods
are imported from outside East Africa, though some are produced locally in Dar es Salaam and some at Jinja in Uganda.
Some clothing and blankets are also produced in Kenya.   The
import of piecegoods is now almost entirely an open trade.
Scarcely any agencies remain.   The former role in this trade
of the general importing house has been taken over mainly by
firms in the bazaar trade. Only a few specialised lines remain
as agency lines with the general importing houses. In the bazaar there are comparatively few large importers, perhaps
about a dozen, but there are literally hundreds who import in
small quantities, many of them only occasionally. Imports
from Japan are normally made through indentors, while those
from India are more often direct. Nyanza Textiles in Uganda
have appointed an exclusive agent, who in turn has appointed

various distributors. One of the producers in Dar es Salaam
has adopted the same policy while the other has merely appointed
several distributors.

The large importers, whose turnover is normally in the range
of $560,000 to $1,400,000 a year, are importers and wholesalers
only. They do not normally sell retail at all. The numerous
small importers on the other hand almost all sell retail as well
as wholesale, and may well buy much of their supplies from the
large importers. The large importers tend to import most of
the fast-moving bulk lines, while the small importers tend to
import special lines as far as possible, buying the fast-moving
lines from the big importers. This is by no means a universal
rule, but it is the tendency.

Outside Dar es Salaam there are few large importers from
overseas: one or two in Tanga and one or two in Mwanza, and
these are of only moderate size. In both Tanga and Mwanza the
merchants tend to obtain most of their supplies from importers
in Mombasa. The firms in Mwanza which import direct normally do so through Dar es Salaam, as freight rates are slightly
lower than from Mombasa. Other than these few firms in Tanga
and Mwanza, there are no large importers of piecegoods from
abroad outside Dar es Salaam. Even the wholesalers in the
ports of Lindi and Mtwara obtain most of their supplies from
Dar es Salaam, though some of the bulk items are shipped direct,
rather than being trans-shipped. Up-country there are, of
course, hundreds of wholesalers, and even retailers, who import small quantities of piecegoods, and particularly clothing,
direct. However, as with the small importers in Dar es Salaam,
they are only importing special lines.

The large importers sell partly to other wholesalers, and
sub-wholesalers in Dar es Salaam, but mostly they sell to wholesalers and sub-wholesalers up-country. The distinction between
importers, wholesalers and sub-wholesalers may seem unneces-
sarily complicated and perhaps artificial, since it has already
been explained how difficult it is to make a realistic distinction
between wholesalers and retailers. However, such a distinction
does exist. In order to reach the most remote areas, goods,
particularly piecegoods, frequently have to pass through four
separate stages in the distribution system: the importer, the
wholesaler, the sub-wholesaler and the retailer. In most cases,
however, one or possibly two of these stages is omitted. In
most areas which are not too remote there are three links in
the chain, importer, wholesaler and retailer, though the links
can be importer, sub-wholesaler and retailer. This may seem
to be a quibble. If a sub-wholesaler is buying direct from an

importer, then surely he is more properly called a whole -
saler. But this is not necessarily so. A sub-wholesaler may
buy most of his supplies from a wholesaler, but in certain
circumstances will buy direct from the importer. This does
not mean that he automatically becomes a wholesaler.   The
diagram below shows the various possible routes in a simpli -
fied form.

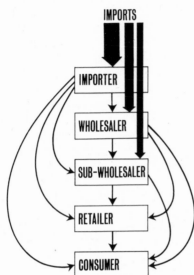

The role of the broker. There is also another intermediary
who has not been mentioned so far and who is not shown in the
diagram. This is the broker, who plays a vital part in the
whole system. There were 52 brokers licensed in Dar es
Salaam in 1961, one in Tanga and one in Mwanza.   There are
also a great many in Mombasa.
     There are four methods by which importers and wholesalers
can sell their goods to up-country traders. The up-country
trader may come down to Dar es Salaam at intervals of varying
frequency and visit the numerous wholesalers and importers,
making his purchases personally. The Dar es Salaam merchant
may send round a traveller with samples who takes orders.
Failing this he may send round by post price lists or some form
of catalogue (seldom if ever illustrated). From these, and as
a result of his previous visits to Dar es Salaam, the up-country
trader can place his orders direct. Finally the up-country
trader can make use of one or more brokers with whom he is
in contact. He will write or telephone to his broker stating his
requirements. The broker will place the order as advantageously
as possible with one or more of the wholesalers in the bazaar.

For this he receives a commission which varies according to
the size of the order and the importance of the client.   The
normal commission is $\frac{1}{4}$ per cent paid by the seller, and that
paid by the buyer varies between nothing and $\frac{1}{2}$ per cent.

A good broker will keep this up-country client informed on
such matters as the general state of the market, any particu -
larly favourable bargains available, future shipments due, etc.
It is of course only a large client who is worth all the trouble
and expense involved in such a service. A bad broker may be
in the pocket of one or more of the wholesalers, he may be less
than energetic in exploring all the multifarious sources of supply in the bazaar or in driving a particularly hard bargain for
his client. A good broker is a great asset. His role in the
distribution system is vital. The great distances in Tangan -
yika, the very large number of suppliers in Dar es Salaam,
the rapid changes in prices and availability of supplies all make
it essential for most wholesalers up-country to employ the ser -
vices of a broker. It is very difficult to make an accurate estimate, but it seems likely that rather more than half of the sales
of piecegoods made by importers and wholesalers to up-country
traders are made through brokers.

The use of travellers. As a corollary to this, comparatively
few Dar es Salaam merchants send travellers round canvassing
up-country, far fewer than the merchants in Mombasa.   There
are various reasons for this. There are more big importers
and wholesalers in Mombasa, and their average size is greater.
They are supplying most of the East African market. Dar es
Salaam wholesalers are supplying only a part of it. This means
that it is worth the while of a Mombasa wholesaler to send out
travellers to cover all three territories, while the Dar es Salaam
wholesaler covering only one, and not all of that, often feels that
the trouble and expense would not be justified. A further ad -
vantage enjoyed by Mombasa merchants is that the season in
Kenya and Uganda is earlier than in Tanganyika, so that they
can spread their period of peak sales, and their travellers can
move on to Tanganyika after covering the other two territories.

Perhaps the most important reason for the large number of
travellers from Mombasa is that there are several large wholesalers there who specialise exclusively in fancy goods, sundries,
cutlery, and similar lines, while in Dar es Salaam there are few
big wholesalers who deal exclusively in these lines. There are
many who deal in them in a rather small way, often in conjunction
with other lines, but these merchants are not able to carry the
large stocks and wide selection of goods which are essential in th
section of the trade. They mostly do not seem to be able to affor

the overhead expenses involved in sending out a traveller.
The position of Dar es Salaam versus Mombasa in the piecegoods trade. Repeatedly, in the course of this survey, it was
stated by wholesalers in all parts of Tanganyika that in fancy
goods and sundries lines prices were appreciably lower in Mombasa than in Dar es Salaam and that the range of goods was very
much greater. We have seen that the Northern and the West
Lake Regions draw most, and the Lake and Tanga Regions a
large part of their supplies from Mombasa. However, the extent
of the penetration by Kenya wholesalers into the rest of the country may not be fully realised. For instance, at Mbozi in the
Southern Highlands Region, 20 miles from the Northern Rhodesia
border, two travellers from Nairobi selling ready-made clothing
pay three or four visits a year. No travellers from Dar es
Salaam had visited Mbozi in recent years, it was said. One of
the largest piecegoods wholesalers in Mbozi stated that he obtained half of all his supplies from Mombasa, some from Nairobi
and the remainder from Dar es Salaam. Even one of the small
sub-wholesalers obtained all his supplies of cutlery from Mombasa.

The trade figures show that the importers at Mombasa have
been increasing their share of the Tanganyika market in recent
years. The table below gives the proportion of the main types
of piecegoods and clothing imported into Tanganyika through
Mombasa in 1956 and in 1961.

THE PROPORTION OF TANGANYIKA'S NET IMPORTS
OF CERTAIN CATEGORIES OF PIECEGOODS AND
CLOTHING PASSING THROUGH MOMBASA
IN 1956 AND 1961

	Per cent	
	1956	1961
Cotton, grey unbleached	22.2	40.5
Cotton, khaki drill	26.3	39.9
Cotton, dyed in the piece	10.2	29.6
Khangas	0.4	1.2
Fabrics of synthetic fibres	4.5	33.3
Blankets and coverlets	21.5	41.0
Clothing	46.8	49.2

Source Annual Trade Reports

In every one of the main categories of textiles imported into Tanganyika, the Mombasa merchants have increased their share of the market. The table on page 79 shows the position and the change in the five-year period in terms of value.

In all these categories where total net imports have increased, the imports through Kenya have increased proportionately more, and when net imports have decreased, imports through Kenya have decreased less or even increased. It may be argued that 1956 and 1961 are not representative years. An examination of the trade figures in other years does not bear this out. The only major difference is in imports of fabrics of synthetic fibres in 1960. The total net imports in that year were worth $4,556,000 of which direct imports were valued at $2,486,000 and imports through Kenya at $2,097,000. This means that in 1960, 45.8 per cent of imports of fabrics of synthetic fibres entered via Kenya, while in 1961 this proportion has been reduced to 33.3 per cent. Otherwise the proportions in other years correspond quite closely to the trend shown in the table.

The categories of textile imports which showed the biggest increases between 1956 and 1961 were khangas, cotton fabrics dyed in the piece other than khaki drill, clothing and blankets. Imports of khaki drill are decreasing and so are those of plain black cloth (not shown). Imports of fabrics of synthetic fibres fluctuate considerably from year to year, but the overall level is more or less unchanged.

The value of total net imports into Tanganyika rose considerably between 1956 and 1961, but the value of direct imports, i.e. those imported by Tanganyika merchants, declined slightly. In other words the increase in imports has been handled by Kenya merchants. The business of the importers of textiles in Tanganyika seems to have been stagnating. It may be argued that local production has taken the place of imports in the Dar es Salaam merchant's turnover. It is true that in 1961 imports of textiles from Uganda and Kenya were valued at almost $1.4 million but this trade was not on the whole handled by merchants in Dar es Salaam, while local production in Dar es Salaam was still equivalent to less than 5 per cent of imports in 1961. There is no doubt that Dar es Salaam textile importers and wholesalers are handling a declining share of the total Tanganyika trade.

The one encouraging point to emerge from the figures in the table on page 79 is the big increase in the trade in khangas, imports of which have almost exactly doubled in the last five year. This increase has been handled almost entirely by Tanganyika importers. However, these importers have some sort of a natural protection in this field. Consumption of khangas outside

THE VALUE OF NET IMPORTS, DIRECT IMPORTS AND IMPORTS ENTERING TANGANYIKA THROUGH KENYA IN 1956 AND 1961

	1956	$ '000 1961	Change
Cotton grey, unbleached			
Net	1,378	1,478	+ 100
Direct	1,072	879	- 193
Through Kenya	305	599	+ 294
Cotton, khaki drill			
Net	938	526	- 412
Direct	692	316	- 376
Through Kenya	246	210	- 36
Cotton, dyed in the piece			
Net	2,190	3,534	+ 1,344
Direct	1,966	2,489	+ 523
Through Kenya	224	1,044	+ 820
Khangas			
Net	1,459	2,934	+ 1,475
Direct	1,453	2,898	+ 1,445
Through Kenya	6	36	+ 30
Fabrics of synthetic fibres			
Net	4,354	3,984	- 370
Direct	4,158	2,660	- 1,498
Through Kenya	196	1,324	+ 1,128
Blankets and coverlets			
Net	1,030	1,159	+ 129
Direct	809	683	- 126
Through Kenya	221	476	+ 255
Clothing			
Net	2,260	2,750	+ 490
Direct	1,201	1,397	+ 196
Through Kenya	1,058	1,352	+ 294

Source   Annual Trade Reports

Tanganyika is negligible, being confined mainly to the Coast
Province of Kenya. The total imports of khangas into Kenya
and Uganda together were valued at less than $280,000 in 1961,
while imports into Tanganyika were worth over $2.8 million.
Even so the Mombasa merchants were able to make some minor
inroads into the khanga market in Tanganyika.

A further examination of the figures in the two tables reveals
one very disquieting fact: Kenya merchants are making the biggest inroads into the Tanganyika market in all the most rapidly
expanding lines except khangas. They are in fact expanding
their share of that part of the market which has the best pros-
pects for the future. They have already captured a very large
part of this market; almost a half of the trade in ready-made
clothing for instance. As incomes rise in Tanganyika the deman
is increasingly for better quality and more varied piecegoods
and for cheap ready-made clothing. In 1956 Kenya supplied only
$224,000 worth, or 10 per cent, of imports of cotton goods dyed
in the piece. By 1961 Kenya was supplying $1.0 million worth,
or almost 30 per cent of the total imports. Kenya merchants
seem to be well on the way to establishing themselves as the chie
importers of textiles for Tanganyika. Dar es Salaam merchants
may some day, in the not very distant future, find themselves
handling only khangas out of the whole range of textile imports,
unless the expansion in production by the textile mills in Dar es
Salaam arrives in time to save their trade. However, if these
mills do grow large enough to supply a sizable part of the market, they are likely to set up their own marketing organisations,
by-passing altogether the existing Dar es Salaam wholesalers.

Clearly the channels of distribution in Dar es Salaam, at any
rate as far as piecegoods are concerned, are not working satisfactorily. Mombasa certainly has various natural advantages,
already enumerated, over Dar es Salaam as a distribution centre for textiles. Nevertheless, it seems clear that there are
steps which the Dar es Salaam merchants could take to improve
their competitive position. As the distribution system is organis
in Tanganyika today, fancy goods and clothing have essentially to
be sold by travellers canvassing wholesalers round the country.
New designs, new fashions and new styles have to be brought to
the notice of the up-country wholesaler. It is no use expecting
him to buy these fashion goods unseen through a broker. Though
the brokerage system plays a vital part in the trade, wholesalers
in Dar es Salaam seem to rely on it far too heavily.

The second weakness of the Dar es Salaam piecegoods wholesalers is their comparatively small size. They are not able to
keep large stocks and they are unable to order from the Japanese

suppliers in large enough quantities to obtain the quantity discounts received by the Mombasa importers. They do not have
a big enough turnover to be able to cut their margins to the
level of the Mombasa merchants. Almost without exception up-
country wholesalers complain that the range of goods in Dar es
Salaam is smaller and the prices are higher than in Mombasa.
There seems to be a strong case for the amalgamation of some
of the Dar es Salaam firms in this line of business. There
should be no question of larger firms obtaining a monopoly position, since there will always be the competition from Mombasa
as long as the customs union exists. The object of a merger
would be to enable the resulting larger businesses to compete
with Mombasa in all parts of Tanganyika, particularly in the
Lake Region, which is by far the largest single market, but
also the one in which Kenya merchants have made the biggest
inroads, and in which they are most likely in the near future to
supplant the Dar es Salaam suppliers completely.
<u>Up-country channels of distribution.</u> Having examined in some
detail the operation of the piecegoods distributors in Dar es
Salaam, it is necessary to consider the succeeding links in the
distributive chain. The simplest way of doing this is to examine
how piecegoods do in fact reach the consumer in different parts
of the country.

At Mbeya, for instance, in the Southern Highlands Region, the
larger wholesalers of piecegoods, with a wholesale turnover of
perhaps $210, 000 to $560, 000 a year, obtain about half of their
supplies from Dar es Salaam, about a fifth each from Mombasa
and Uganda - Jinja textiles are very popular in the area - and
about a tenth by direct import from abroad. Wholesalers of this
sort normally sell mainly piecegoods, though they also deal in
other lines in a smaller way, such as provisions, hardware and
sundries. In addition they do a certain amount of retail business,
perhaps worth $45, 000 to $140, 000 a year, $140, 000 being pro-
bably the largest retail turnover in these lines in the town.

A small sub-wholesaler in Mbeya might have a turnover of
between $14, 000 and $28, 000 a year, half retail and half wholesale, split between piecegoods, clothing, sundries and cutlery.
His supplies come almost equally from Dar es Salaam and
Mombasa, he makes use of a broker in each, while some supplies
are also obtained from Nairobi or locally from wholesalers in
Mbeya. The trader we are considering is dealing in comparatively
high-quality goods for the better-off African consumers. These
items he buys in fairly small quantities from the wholesalers in
Dar es Salaam or Mombasa, who usually import them direct.
The cheaper and slightly more fast-moving lines he buys, again

in not very large quantities - certainly never as much as a bale
at a time - from wholesalers who do not import direct, either
locally or from Dar es Salaam. This trader is therefore   a
typical border-line case between wholesaler and sub-wholesaler
who is at the same time doing half of his business as a retailer.

At Ngomba, a fishing village on the shore of Lake Rukwa,
just under 100 miles from Mbeya in Chunya District, there are
perhaps 15 or 20 small African shops. The area is quite prosperous, deriving its cash income from the lake fishing industry.
A typical small shopkeeper, selling foodstuffs, sundries and
piecegoods and employing a tailor to make up clothing, buys his
supplies in Mbeya, going in once a week by bus. He does not
buy in Chunya, where there are several small sub-wholesalers,
even though it is on his way to Mbeya, being only 57 miles
against 92 miles to Mbeya. The Chunya sub-wholesalers obtain
most of their supplies from Mbeya, so that for the trader in
Ngomba who has a big enough turnover to cover the extra bus
fare, it is cheaper to buy direct from the wholesalers in Mbeya.

A contrast to this is presented by an African trader at Ipinda,
about 10 miles from the northern shore of Lake Nyasa in Rungwe
District. This trader has quite a large turnover, but obtains
almost all his supplies from the wholesalers in Tukuyu, which
is about 36 miles away, and also on his road to Mbeya, which is
about 80 miles away. Tukuyu is a very much bigger place than
Chunya, which is now practically a ghost town after the aban-
donment of the Lupa Goldfields. The wholesalers in Tukuyu
obtain all their supplies direct from Dar es Salaam and Mombasa.
In several cases they have as large a turnover as the wholesalers
in Mbeya. Therefore, the trader at Ipinda, unlike his counter-
part at Ngomba, gains no advantage from travelling the extra
45 miles to Mbeya.

At Kilwa in the Southern Region a different pattern and set of
problems emerge. At Kilwa Kivinje there are only six or seven
wholesalers. They all deal in all the lines sold locally, are all
both wholesalers and retailers and their average turnover is each
in the region of $140,000 a year, some less, some more. Their
supplies of piecegoods are obtained from Dar es Salaam, by road
in the dry season, by dhow in the rains, when the flooding of the
Rufiji River makes the road to Dar es Salaam impassable. Most
of their supplies of foodstuffs on the other hand are obtained from
Lindi. In Kilwa District there are six trading centres of any
importance. Each of the wholesalers has a branch in each centre. The branch is normally managed by an African, who receives
a salary. In the larger trading centres the branch acts as a
sub-wholesaler selling to small shops in the surrounding area.

However, all but the very smallest window-shops obtain their
supplies direct from the wholesalers in Kilwa.

The position of branch shops. Branch shops are common in
trading centres throughout the Southern Region; though, rather
than being wholly-owned branches with a salaried manager, as
in Kilwa District, it is more usual for branches in other districts
to be run by an African who receives all his supplies on credit
from one wholesaler. He does not receive a salary, but has to
make his own trading profit. The difference between the two systems is not very great in practice. There are also a good many
wholesalers in Lindi, who have branches in one or more of the
various main centres in the Southern Region, such as Newala,
Masasi or Songea. These branches in turn operate smaller
branches in the surrounding areas. Two of the wholesalers in
Kilwa, for instance, are branches with their head offices in Lindi.

This system of branch shops is more highly developed and extensive in the Southern Region than elsewhere. Its object is to
facilitate the buying of local produce and only secondarily to distribute consumer goods. (This question of the connection between
produce trading and distributive trading is examined more closely
below). The system used to be very much more widespread than
it is today. It was very common in the Lake Region, for instance,
but now only a few branch shops survive. When the marketing
of produce is taken over by the co-operatives, the system of
branch shops at once begins to wither. If the primary purpose
of buying local produce from the growers is removed, it seldom
remains worth the trader's while to maintain his branches just
for the distribution of consumer goods. The turnover is not
usually large enough to justify the trouble and expense. The
main problem is the cost of supervising the branch and the losses
suffered if this supervision is not very close.

In 1961, the Southern Region was the only region remaining
where the major cash crops of the area, cashew and cassave,
were not marketed by co-operatives, but were still handled by
the produce dealers. In the Northern, Lake, West Lake and Southern Highlands Regions the principal cash crops are all marketed
by co-operatives, and scarcely any branch shops remain, while
in the Tanga and Eastern Regions the main crops are produced on
estates, and there never has been a well-developed system of
branch shops. In the Central and Western regions there are no
major cash crops but a variety of minor ones, such as maize,
millet, paddy, tobacco, groundnuts, sunflower and castor seed,
hides and skins and beeswax. These are still almost entirely
handled by the produce dealers, who maintain a system of branches
in these regions. It is not so well-developed as in the Southern

Region, mainly, it seems, because the system of buying produce by auction in local markets has been in force, and it is
generally simpler for the produce buyer to send round an
agent who buys, rather than go to the expense of maintaining
a large number of permanent branches in the various market
centres. Branch shops are also well-established in Musoma
and North Mara Districts, where the local produce, hedge
sisal, ghee, maize, wembe and hides and skins, is not handled
by co-operatives.

Seasonal variations in the channels of distribution. To return
to Kilwa District, the trade of a fair-sized African shop in a
centre about 60 miles from Kilwa and about 35 to 40 miles
from the main road provides an interesting illustration of some
aspects of how the channels of distribution operate. This shop
has an annual turnover of about $7,000 and is one of the biggest
in those parts. It sells supplies in very small quantities to
five or six window-shops in the surrounding area. It also buys
some local produce. As in the rest of Kilwa District, sales
are almost entirely of piecegoods, clothing and a few sundry
items such as cigarettes, soap, razor blades, patent medicines,
torch and radio batteries. Hardly any foodstuffs are sold, as
these are all grown locally. The exceptions are sugar, salt,
tinned milk, tea and the like.

Supplies are normally obtained from the wholesalers in Kilwa
Kivinje by road. However, during the rains the road is impassable, and supplies are taken by dhow about 15 miles up the coast.
From there they are carried by porters in 60 lb. head loads a
distance of 40 to 50 miles. This costs approximately $2 a load.
It does not add very greatly to the price of piecegoods, in any
case few if any are bought during the rainy season, but it does
add considerably to the price of foodstuffs and kerosene. It is
of course during the rains and before the harvest that demand
for foodstuffs is greatest. The normal trend in the Southern
Region is for the price of piecegoods to rise during the produce
season, roughly June to December, and for the price of foodstuffs
to rise steeply in January to March or April.

During the first half of the season, from June to October,
when the road is open, the African shop we are considering
sends a hired lorry direct to Dar es Salaam. This takes produce
to be sold, while at the same time supplies are bought from the
wholesalers, thus by-passing the wholesalers in Kilwa.   The
prices paid are naturally very much lower in Dar es Salaam than
in Kilwa. However, this direct trading with Dar es Salaam can
only be undertaken when the road is open, when the quantities to
be sold and bought are enough to cover the cost of transport and

when the necessary finance is available.

Extended chain of distribution in remote areas. Turning to
Ngara District in the West Lake Region, we find that the chain
of distribution there is an extended one, and that there are few
chances of shortening it, as the distances involved are so great.
The owner of a small African shop has little choice but to ob -
tain his supplies from a sub-wholesaler at some local centre
such as Ngara or Rulenge. The nearest large wholesalers are
at Bukoba or Mwanza, some 180 to 200 miles away. The sub-
wholesaler in Ngara or Rulenge does not have a big enough turnover or resources to enable him to obtain his supplies direct
from the coast, and he is dependent on wholesalers in Bukoba,
Mwanza or possibly Shinyanga, who, in turn, obtain most of
their supplies direct from the importers. Similar problems
exist in other remote districts such as Ufipa, Kasulu and Kibondo and also in Mbulu, which, though not so far from the coast,
tends to be isolated.

Most of the retail shops in Mbulu District in Northern Region
are small and obtain their supplies from sub-wholesalers at
Mbulu, Karatu or Babati. Some of the larger ones, however,
during the season - when turnover is very much greater - ob -
tain their supplies from the wholesalers in Arusha; this is where
the sub-wholesalers make most of their purchases, though bulk
items, such as cement and corrugated iron sheets, are obtained
direct from Mombasa, while certain special lines, such as motor
spares, are obtained from Nairobi.

In Arusha the piecegoods wholesalers obtain probably two -
thirds of their supplies from the Mombasa importers and the remainder is split fairly evenly between direct importers or wholesalers in Dar es Salaam and Nairobi. Supplies from Dar es
Salaam are restricted almost entirely to khangas.

In Moshi there is rather an unusual situation in the piecegoods
trade, which brings out very clearly the importance of seasonal
factors in the shaping of channels of distribution. There is only
one large piecegoods wholesaler in Moshi; he obtains all his
supplies from Mombasa, where his head office is located. There
are perhaps twenty-five other wholesalers, whose turnovers
range between perhaps $56,000 and $210,000 a year. In the season, when total sales in the district more than double, these
wholesalers buy direct from Mombasa. However, during the
slack period when sales are very low, they mostly obtain their
supplies from the one big wholesaler in the town. In the season
a wholesaler normally requires a whole bale of americani, which
he obtains from Mombasa. In the slack season he wants only four
or five pieces, which he buys locally. This shows clearly a factor

which affects trade throughout the country. During the season,
when trade is enormously expanded, sometimes to three or
four times its normal volume, the number of links in the dis -
tributive chain is reduced. In the slack season the number is
increased.

The difference in the volume of trade in and out of season
is so great that a different pattern of trade emerges. In the
season, quite small sub-wholesalers are able to place orders
big enough to be of interest to the importers, while small
retailers can often by-pass the sub-wholesalers and go direct
to the wholesaler.

Another example of this is to be found in the southern part
of Mwanza District. At Misungwi, 30 miles south of Mwanza,
there are about 25 traders, of whom four or five are whole -
salers. There are about 200 African shops in the area. When
demand is slack these mostly obtain their supplies from Mi -
sungwi, but when sales rise during the season many of them
buy from wholesalers in Mwanza. On the other hand, of the
wholesalers in Misungwi, the two or three smaller ones obtain
their supplies all the year round from Mwanza, while the two
larger ones obtain much of theirs direct from Dar es Salaam
and Mombasa during the season. These two wholesalers are
each in the habit of sending round a lorry to the small retailers
in the area, wholesaling from the lorry, while at the same time
collecting the local produce such as gram, groundnuts, paddy
and hedge sisal. This practice counteracts the tendency for the
retailers to buy their supplies in Mwanza during the season,
and increases the turnover of the two Misungwi wholesalers
enough to enable them to order direct from Dar es Salaam and
Mombasa.

Differing channels for fast- and slow-moving lines. There is
one aspect of the piecegoods trade which has not perhaps been
brought out very clearly in the discussion so far. In this trade,
as in most others, there is a small selection of fast-moving
lines, and there is also a much larger selection of rather more
slow-moving and usually more expensive lines. The channels
of distribution for these two types of goods are often rather
different. Some firms tend to specialise in importing the fast-
moving lines, others the slow-moving fancy lines. It is in this
second field that the multitude of small importers and whole -
salers tends to operate. Some of the lines may need a certain
amount of specialised trading knowledge. The margins on them
are much bigger and, if an exclusive line can be found, there is
a chance of making a killing. Many of the fancy lines are not
imported into Tanganyika in such quantities that bulk discounts

are a significant factor. This is particularly the case when
there are so many small importers, making it almost impossible for any one or two to build up a big enough trade to reap the
advantages of bulk discounts. Entry to this trade is very easy.
Very little capital is needed, as almost all the goods can be obtained on credit. Hence the multiplicity of small importers of
the fancy clothing and sundries lines, not only in Dar es Salaam,
but all over Tanganyika.

The fast-moving and the slow-moving lines tend to be imported
through different channels, but they are mostly both bought ultimately by the consumer from the same retail shop. Most shops
selling piecegoods stock the fast-moving lines and a selection
of the slow-moving ones. There are, of course, retail shops
which specialise in one line or the other, but these are exceptional. The point in the distribution system at which the two
lines merge varies. It may be at the import, wholesale, sub-
wholesale or retail level. Usually it is at the wholesale level.
For one thing many wholesalers import these lines direct, to
add to the fast-moving lines they buy from Dar es Salaam. The
distributive chain tends to be shorter for slow-moving lines.
They are imported by traders further down the chain, and retailers tend to obtain their supplies of them direct from small
importers, rather than through wholesalers or sub-wholesalers.
The few retailers catering for the European market in clothing
and textiles almost all import most of their supplies direct from
abroad, while the rest they buy from wholesalers in Nairobi.

Provisions

Under the heading of provisions are included local produce
distributed inside Tanganyika as well as what in England would
be called groceries and provisions. The produce forms the
fast-moving, bulk section of the trade; provisions are normally
more slow-moving and imported, though there are exceptions
to this. Soap is locally produced and fast-moving, while sugar
is fast-moving also, though about half of it was imported until
1962. Tinned milk is imported and can, in some areas, be quite
a fast-moving line. Groceries, as understood in Tanganyika,
is a rather specialised trade, catering mainly for the European
and better-off Asian market and dealing almost exclusively in
imported lines.

This diversity in the provisions trade is one of the factors
which make this sector of the distribution network rather complex. Another is the geographical diversity of the sources of
supply. Produce is obtained from all parts of the country. Very
little of the bulk commodities in the provisions trade is imported,
so that Dar es Salaam is the point of origin of only a small part

of the total supplies, in contrast to the situation in the piecegoods trade. Finally the close connection between produce -
buying from the growers, its distribution to the consumers and
its export abroad adds to the complexity of the network.

Produce bought from the growers in any one district is seldom bought by consumers in that district, except by those living
in the towns, and occasionally by people in the rural areas in
the period before the next harvest, when supplies run short. In
this latter case supplies are normally imported back into the
district from outside, as few local traders hold large stocks
from one harvest almost to the next against the chance of a
shortage. Produce therefore normally passes by various channels into the hands of the fairly small number of large produce
dealers in the main centre of any particular area. These dealers usually perform four separate distributive functions, and
very often a fifth as well. They buy the local produce, they
then either export it abroad or they send it to another part of
East Africa. They buy produce from other areas and wholesale
it locally. They very often combine produce trading with some
other trade, most usually the wholesaling of piecegoods, though
often also of building materials. In addition to all this, many
of the large dealers are also millers of maize, rice or oil.

Not all produce by any means is channelled through the large
dealers. Many wholesalers who are not primarily produce dea
lers also buy produce. Occasionally they may export it themselves or send it to Dar es Salaam to be exported. On the othe
hand, they may sell it to produce buyers in other areas for con
sumption in these areas, or they may do a deal with wholesaler
in other areas who are also in the produce business in only a
small way like themselves.

A large proportion of the main crops not handled by the co-
operatives is handled by the big produce dealers. There are
normally between four and six in a main centre such as Dodoma
Tabora, Mwanza, Arusha or Lindi. In Dar es Salaam there ar
of course more. The reason for the rather small number of
big dealers is that considerable capital is required for this
business.

The biggest produce dealers do not normally deal also in im
ported provisions, which are often agency lines, imported by
the larger importing houses. The big local millers in Dar es
Salaam have also appointed agents. Other imported provisions
lines, for instance most brands of tinned milk, biscuits and
sweets, are ordered through indentors.

The smaller produce dealers often deal in provisions lines
as well. Such dealers are combining the functions of both prod

dealers and provisions wholesalers. The provisions wholesaler as such normally buys his produce requirements from a big produce dealer, either locally or in Dar es Salaam or more usually in the areas where the produce concerned is grown. He buys his provisions requirements from the importers in Dar es Salaam or imports them direct through indentors.

Much of the demand for provisions is located in the towns and in areas where there are plantations, since this is where large numbers of wage-earners are found, who buy most of their food requirements for cash rather than grow them themselves. In these areas where the turnover is considerable, the provisions wholesalers normally sell direct to the retailers.

In the rural areas many of the retailers buy their supplies of provisions direct from the wholesalers in the towns or large trading centres. However, many retailers are either too far from the towns, or their turnover is too small. These retailers buy in the local trading centre from the sub-wholesalers, who are almost invariably also selling retail. At this level the pattern of distribution of provisions is very similar to that of piece-goods. The sub-wholesaler, outside the very largest towns, is normally a general store selling all types of goods, mainly piece-goods and provisions, both retail and also wholesale to the small shops in the surrounding rural areas.

Main produce dealing centres. Dar es Salaam does not occupy such a unique position in the provisions trade as in the piecegoods trade, as a much smaller proportion of the total turnover is imported. The biggest imported lines are sugar, $2.25 million worth in 1961, tinned milk in various forms, $1.8 million, kerosene $1.14 million, wines and spirits $720,000, soaps etc. $355,000 and matches $347,000. These mostly pass through Dar es Salaam. Much of the wheat flour is produced by mills in Dar es Salaam and marketed there, though there are also mills at Arusha and Iringa. The large maize mills are likewise in Dar es Salaam though there are a good many medium-sized mills in other parts of the country, and literally hundreds of small ones.

The biggest produce dealers are in Dar es Salaam as they handle most of the produce exports. The Dar es Salaam area is probably the biggest single market for provisions, though the combined consumption of Tanga and Lushoto Districts, where so many estates are located, is very high, as is that of Morogoro District. Dar es Salaam has a certain entrepot trade in produce, mostly in lines from the Southern Region to the rest of the country; cassava, beans and peas, sorghum and rice, and also rice from the Rufiji District.

A good deal of the provisions lines imported from Kenya
pass through Dar es Salaam, though by no means all. Arusha
and Mwanza are important distribution centres for these products. The most important items imported from the other two
territories (excluding beer and cigarettes) were, in 1961: tea
$1, 294, 400, soap etc. $1, 386, 000 ($154, 000 from Uganda),
butter $431, 200, biscuits $386, 400 ($106, 400 from Uganda),
roasted coffee $204, 400 and sweets $168, 000 ($92, 400 from
Uganda).

After Dar es Salaam, Mwanza is probably the next largest
distribution centre for produce and provisions. The local mar
ket in the Lake Region is very large. Many of the local farmer
concentrate on growing cash crops, and buy the food supplies
from outside sources. This is the beginning of a break-throug
into a fully cash economy, and in sharp contrast to most other
areas. There is no wheat milling in Mwanza, though there is a
big cottonseed oil milling industry in the area. A considerable
entrepot trade between the Lake Region and Kenya and Uganda
passes through Mwanza.

Specialised provisions lines. There are a good many rather
specialised channels of distribution for various particular lines
within the general provisions category. Groceries in Tanganyika are normally distributed by fairly specialised retailers
catering for a rather small market. A few of their lines are
the same as those handled by the general provisions retailers,
but mostly they are tinned goods and the like, with only a very
limited market. These are obtained either from importers wit
agencies, or often imported direct, frequently through indentor
Previously the importers distributed many of these lines throu
wholesalers in Dar es Salaam. Now they tend to cut these out
and distribute direct to the wholesalers and retailers, mainly
retailers, up-country. The former wholesalers have taken to
importing the non-agency lines themselves and also to obtainin
agencies as far as possible. Those retailers up-country who
have a very small turnover in groceries, in district centres fo
instance, tend to buy most of their supplies from the few Dar e
Salaam wholesalers in these lines. These wholesalers usually
import most of their supplies direct and obtain some from ager
they usually also have retail grocery stores in Dar es Salaam.

Wines and spirits are mostly imported by agents and distri
buted direct to the wholesaler/retailers up-country. There ar
a few specialised wines and spirits retailers in Dar es Salaam
and one or two in the main towns. Otherwise these lines are
distributed by grocers and some provisions retailers.

Almost all the beer consumed in Tanganyika is brewed in Ea

Africa. In 1961 there was one brewery in Dar es Salaam, while $1.57 million worth of beer was imported from Kenya and $123,000 worth from Uganda. The breweries have a fairly extensive network of their own depots, from which they supply appointed distributors in the various districts, who have to fulfil certain requirements over the provision of transport, etc.

Only $81,000 worth of cigarettes, cigars, pipe tobacco and snuff were imported into Tanganyika from abroad. Almost all the cigarettes consumed are manufactured in East Africa, some at the factory in Dar es Salaam, but mostly in Kenya and Uganda. Tanganyika imported $3.1 million worth of cigarettes from Kenya in 1961 and $1.2 million from Uganda. The distributive network for cigarettes is probably the most highly organised and controlled in Tanganyika. The whole country is divided into seven sales districts, with one of the company's own sales representatives in charge of each. A hierarchy of distributors and dealers has been established, all with carefully defined areas. Rigid conditions and terms are laid down. A blanket coverage of the country has been achieved with uniform prices throughout. Very careful control of stock is exercised by constant visits and checks on all distributors. The threat of withdrawing supplies from any dealer or retailer who fails to comply with the stipulated conditions, with the knowledge that no alternative supply exists, is a very powerful weapon in the hands of the manufacturer.

We have seen that very few piecegoods wholesalers operate a network of branches, though a few have one or two branches besides their main place of business. More produce dealers and provisions wholesalers tend to have branches, even if the small branches designed to buy produce from the growers are discounted. More produce dealers have one or two large branches, though seldom more, carrying on a full-scale wholesaling business. In particular there is a tendency for the Dar es Salaam dealers to have one or two up-country branches. There are obvious advantages in this, particularly when it comes to exporting produce, but also for the up-country branch when obtaining supplies.

The channels of distribution of provisions are on the whole less affected by seasonal changes than those of piecegoods. Most provisions lines being comparatively bulky and requiring adequate storage facilities, it is not easy to change the channels through which they are distributed. The major items most affected by seasonal variations are probably beer and cigarettes, and both these have well organised networks which operate on the same basis throughout the year. Sugar is also affected considerably in many areas, since its main use is often for the brewing of

pombe. Thus, during the season, when turnover is faster,
some of the sub-wholesalers dealing in sugar may be by-passed
In the towns and on estates, where the market for foodstuffs is
largest, the season makes little difference to the volume consumed. In rural areas, where foodstuffs are bought to supplement locally grown produce, the increase in demand is normall
greatest in the out-of-season period, during the rains and befor
the harvest. However, the increase in the quantities consumed
is seldom enough to affect the channels of distribution, except
occasionally to enable the larger retailers to by-pass the sub-
wholesalers.

The transport of provisions. Transport problems are of cours
much greater in the produce and provisions trades than in the
piecegoods trade. A wholesaler who is supplied by rail and can
not order in wagon-loads is unlikely to be able to compete with
a wholesaler with a big enough turnover to enable him to do this
In a country where the distances are so great, transport costs
have a big influence on the patterns of trade. The initial price
of the produce is likely to be less important than the cost of
transport, and one of the main considerations is the ability to
provide a return load.

At the sub-wholesale and retail level the transporting of sacl
of sugar, rice, flour, beans etc., from wholesaler to retailer
in the rural areas can be quite a problem. Usually it is done by
bus, but in some areas several retailers may get together to
hire a lorry or pick-up. In other areas some of the wholesaler
take round supplies by lorry to the retailers. This practice is
not however as common as might be supposed. Comparatively
few wholesalers do it, and mostly not all the year round. The
practice is common only in fairly limited areas.

There are a great many problems associated with establishin
a delivery system of this type. First it must be realised that
when taking round supplies in this way, the wholesaler is not
delivering on the basis of firm orders. He is hawking round his
stock on spec. There is normally no way for a small retailer
in the rural areas to transmit an order, even if he had the fore-
sight to do so. The wholesaler's lorries are seldom able to
keep to a schedule, so that the retailer has no idea when they
are likely to arrive, and frequently has no cash on hand to make
any purchases. The expenses of sending round a lorry are con-
derable. In addition to the obvious ones, a reliable man has to
accompany the lorry and conduct the business. Few wholesaler
are happy unless a member of the family takes part in the expe-
dition. Losses from pilferage can be heavy, and in some areas
wholesalers carrying valuable stocks fear violence. In general

it is not possible to cover the high overhead costs unless the
turnover is quite sizable. In most areas the population is
sparse and scattered over large distances, and one small duka
may be five or ten miles from the next, and even where there
are several retailers their average purchases probably do not
amount to more than perhaps $2.8 per trip, or $7 at the most.
This means that a great many have to be visited, and a very
large mileage run up.

Lorries are only sent round in fairly densely populated
areas, where cash incomes are reasonably high. As might be
expected the practice is most common in the Lake Region, in
particular in Geita District, where there is no convenient local
trading centre, and where the bus services are poor. In areas
where the bus services cover the country fully, lorries are
not sent round by wholesalers. This applies in both Moshi and
Tanga Districts. Other areas where one or two wholesalers
send round lorries are Arusha, Tukuyu in the Southern High -
lands, Musoma in the Lake Region and Mtwara and Newala
in the Southern Region.

It is seldom economic to send round a lorry unless it is able
to carry on more than one type of business. In many places
the wholesaler who is the distributor for one of the breweries
is obliged to send round delivering beer , and he normally
combines this with selling other lines. In other areas selling
foodstuffs or piecegoods is combined with buying, or at any
rate collecting, produce. Few wholesalers send round lorries
except in the season unless they are obliged to do so. Out of
season the turnover is not enough to cover the overheads. In
a few areas where the demand for provisions rises out of season, particularly in the rains, it is worthwhile sending round
Land-Rovers or other four-wheel drive vehicles to otherwise
inaccessible areas, as the prices obtained at these times are
extremely high.

Building materials and hardware

In this section of the trade there is a very sharp distinction
between, on the one hand, the bulk items with a rapid turnover,
such as cement, corrugated iron sheets and, to a lesser extent,
round iron bars, and on the other hand the slow-moving lines
in the way of builders' and decorators' supplies, tools, etc.
The first are all bulky items. Most of the cement supplies are
obtained from Kenya and are distributed by four importing houses
and one specialist importer and wholesaler of building supplies.
Two or three other firms import cement from other sources.
C.I. sheets and round iron bars are imported by a variety of
firms, mostly in the bazaar. Paints, both locally manufactured

and imported, are handled by agents and appointed distributors.
Some builders' supplies are agency lines, others are imported
by the fairly small number of firms in Dar es Salaam who specialise in this trade. Some supplies are imported direct by
wholesalers up-country.

There are comparatively few traders in Tanganyika who
handle building materials. Outside Dar es Salaam there are
usually only one or two firms in each of the main towns. They
obtain their cement from the general importing houses, their
C.I. sheets and round iron bars from the Dar es Salaam or
Mombasa importers and their builders' and decorators' supplie
from either the firms with agencies, the specialist importers o
by direct import. These up-country wholesalers normally sell
direct to the consumers, that is to building contractors, missions, local government authorities, estates or private individuals. Cement and C.I. sheets and a small selection of tools,
paints etc. are sold to sub-wholesalers or retailers. Various
wholesalers who do not otherwise deal in building materials
also handle cement and C.I. sheets, which they obtain from Dar
es Salaam or Mombasa.

Hardware, ironmongery and household items are imported
by either agents, building and hardware merchants or general
sundries importers. Outside Dar es Salaam there are scarcel
any firms who specialise entirely in these lines. They are nor
mally handled as sundries by traders who deal in them along
with their main lines of either piecegoods or provisions.

Chemists goods

Pharmaceuticals are almost all sold to hospitals. They are
imported through the Crown Agents or locally appointed agents.
The market outside the hospitals is very small indeed. The
firms in Dar es Salaam handling the agencies normally send
round travellers selling to the up-country retailers. A very
large part of the business is for orders of less than $14.   The
overhead expenses involved in distributing such small quantitie
of a great variety of different items are very high.

These lines are handled by a very small number of retailers
Outside Dar es Salaam there are very few towns where there is
more than one specialist chemist's shop. Medicines which can
be obtained without a doctor's prescription, patent medicines
and toilet preparations are frequently stocked by grocers or eve
haberdashers catering mainly for the European trade. A selection of patent medicines is normally included among sundries
by wholesalers who deal in this line. Drugs and toilet preparations are normally obtained from the agents or by direct import
Patent medicines are also obtained from agents or from sundri

importers and wholesalers in Dar es Salaam. An assortment
of aspirin-based cure-alls, tonics, purgatives, gripe waters
and rubs are stocked by many of the smallest retailers in rural
areas. These are either obtained from wholesalers or sub-
wholesalers, or certain of them are distributed by van to the
remotest retailers in the country by representatives of the manufacturers, who are usually attached to the importing house that
acts as agent. These vans ensure the widest possible distribution of the products concerned. Supplies in theory pass through
the hands of the wholesaler, who obtains his margin on the
sales, but most of the selling is done by the company's representatives touring round by van.

Consumer durables

Consumer durables, such as bicycles, radios and electrical
goods, are almost all imported by agents, often the large importing houses. These distribute the goods through their branches
and usually also through appointed distributors, sometimes exclusive, sometimes not. The networks are seldom very tightly
organised. The distributors usually sell both retail and on a
sub-wholesaling basis to other retailers. These lines are not
often sold by retailers outside the towns and trading centres,
though occasionally radios are sold by a larger retailer in the
more prosperous and densely populated rural areas.

The motor trade

Cars are imported and distributed by exclusive agents, who
are either purely motor dealers, or by departments of the big
importing houses. These concerns usually have at least three
or four branches, and they appoint dealers in the main centres
where they themselves are not established. Motor spares are
handled by the various agents as well as by a few specialist
firms. Up-country a good many traders carry small stocks
of the most commonly required spares and are prepared to order
others as required from the specialist wholesalers.

Petroleum products

Petroleum products are imported by the oil companies through
Dar es Salaam, Tanga and Mtwara. The West Lake Region is
supplied from Mombasa via Kisumu. The oil companies maintain depots throughout the country. In some areas depots are
operated by agents. From the depots petrol, oil and kerosene
are distributed to service stations and pumps, kerosene also to
wholesalers in four gallon tins. Gas oil, diesel oil and fuel oil
are normally delivered to large consumers direct. All outlets
of any importance are tied outlets.

Capital goods

Capital goods are imported and usually sold direct to the

customer by an agent or manufacturer's representative. Most firms carry a number of exclusive agency lines. For certain lines travellers are sent round and for lines such as agricultural machinery sub-agents are often appointed in the up-country centres.

THE EXTENT OF RETAILING ACTIVITIES
BY WHOLESALERS

It has already become clear that the extent of retailing activities by wholesalers in Tanganyika is very considerable. Practically all the large and small importing houses do a sizabl part of their business direct with the consumer. A few of the very largest wholesalers in Dar es Salaam do no retail business Outside Dar es Salaam there are practically no wholesalers whc do not also sell retail. Those few who are purely wholesalers are almost all big produce dealers.

It is impossible to make an accurate estimate of the extent of retailing by wholesalers in terms of turnover without a comprehensive survey of distribution covering the whole country. However, it is possible to make some very rough estimates. The large wholesalers in Dar es Salaam or up-country often have quite extensive retail sales, sometimes up to $112,000 a year, but more often in the region of $28-56,000 a year. This is usually not more than a quarter and sometimes only a tenth of their total turnover. The smaller wholesalers often do as much as half of their business in the form of retail sales, which may be in the region of $14-56,000 a year. The retail sales of sub-wholesalers, mostly located in trading centres and minor settlements, are frequently more than half of their total turnove Their retail sales may be between $5,600 and $28,000 a year, but not usually more than $14,000 a year.

It seems probable that about one-third of all the retail sales of consumer goods are made by importers, wholesalers or sub-wholesalers; thus about two-thirds of all retail sales are probably made across the counters of traders who are purely retailers.

THE VALUE OF TURNOVER
BY MAIN TYPES OF OUTLETS

As we have already seen, there is practically no specialisa-

tion by types of business. Specialist shops which could be classified as, for instance, grocers, chemists, clothing stores, electrical shops or the like, form only an infinitesimal fraction of
the total number of traders. It is quite impossible to make any
estimates of turnover by different types of outlet, and it would
be totally unrealistic to attempt to do so.

It was estimated earlier that approximately $159.6 million
worth of consumer goods at duty paid prices entered the commercial distribution system in 1961. It seems probable that foodstuffs and groceries, excluding drink and tobacco, formed about
24 per cent of the trade, while piecegoods and clothing, including the cost of making-up by local tailors, came to about 22 per
cent. Other important trades were drink and tobacco, sundry
provisions, of which soap is the most important, building materials, petrol and kerosene and the motor trade.

Although it is not possible to give estimates of the value of
turnover by types of outlet, it is possible to give some indication of the scale of operations of the average importer, wholesaler, sub-wholesaler, and retailer of various sorts. It would
of course be more useful to be able to make estimates of the
number of traders in each turnover category, but this must wait
on the completion of a comprehensive survey of distribution. Any
estimates made on the basis of the present inquiry would be little
more than a guess, and could serve no useful purpose. However,
it does seem worth providing an indication of the order of size
we are dealing with when discussing the various categories of
traders.

The large importing houses mostly have a turnover of somewhere between $560,000 and $2.8 million a year, though a few
have more than this. There are also a good many firms dealing
in agency lines whose turnover is much less, sometimes as
little as $40,000.

The large wholesalers and importers in the bazaar have sales
which range between $560,000 and $2,100,000. Few have more
than this, though it must be remembered that this survey does
not cover those dealing solely in produce-buying and exporting.
Some produce exporters may well have a turnover of more than
$2,100,000.

Below the category of big bulk importers there is a large class
of small and medium-sized wholesalers in Dar es Salaam who
import most, if not all, of their supplies. Their sales vary
between say $56,000 and $560,000. The small wholesalers in
this group are mostly importing various specialised lines, so
that their sales are small, but their margins are comparatively
high. Below them again are the really small wholesalers and

sub-wholesalers who buy most of their supplies locally from the big importers, though not all of them. Their turnover may be between $14,000 and $56,000 a year.

Outside Dar es Salaam there is a small class of big whole-salers in all the main centres, whose turnover is between $560,000 and $1,400,000. Few are much bigger than this. There is a much larger category of medium-sized wholesalers in the range of $140,000 to $560,000 a year, most of them being in the lower half of this range. These wholesalers are mostly in the main centres in each region, but in the Lake Region, in particular, a few of them may be found in the minor centres such as Ngudu or Malampaka. Wholesalers with a turnover smaller than about $140,000 are normally dealing in the more specialist lines in the towns, such as electrical goods or bicycles

Sub-wholesalers, some in the towns, but mostly in the trading centres and minor settlements, usually have sales in the range of $14,000 to $28,000 a year, but some go up to perhaps $70,000 and others down to as little as $8,400 or $11,200 a year. Normally a good half of the sales of these traders is retail, direct to the consumer.

The annual sales of the average small Asian and Arab retailer are usually between $5,600 and $16,800. Very few have sales of more than $16,800 a year, unless they are also sub-whole-saling or else have several tailors making-up clothing as part of their business. Not many have a turnover of less than $5,600 a year, though some of the Arab retailers may. The average annual turnover of Asian and Arab retailers is somewhere between $7,000 and $9,800.

Among African retailers it is very exceptional indeed to find a turnover of more than $11,200 a year. The reasonably well-run and successful African retailer in the African area of a town or in a fairly prosperous rural area usually has a turnover of between $2,800 and $7,000 a year. There are also thousands of small shops with a turnover of between $560 and $1,400 a year. Some window-shops and part-time shops, or those that are only open in the season, may have an even smaller turnover.

There tend to be relatively few African shops with a turnover of between about $1,400 and $2,800. This gap represents a fairly real hurdle for the African retailer who is trying to expand. The smaller shop with a turnover of up to $28 a week sells only the simple day-to-day requirements, such as sugar, salt, kerosene, cigarettes, matches, tea and soap. His stock is quite small - it need not exceed $35 and a sack of sugar represents the largest item. However, in order to do a bigger business than this it is necessary to carry a much wider selection of goods

It is then possible to attract a wider circle of customers than those who live locally and use the shop merely for their small daily requirements. But to do this a very much bigger invest ment in stock is required. At once it becomes necessary to stock a range of five to ten different foodstuffs. There normally have to be bought in sacks or four-gallon tins, and each will cost anything between $4 and $21. In many areas, if a bigger business is to be done it is necessary to stock piecegoods and khangas, and very likely to employ a tailor for at least part of the year. The capital required soon runs into thousands of shillings. From this it will be seen that there is a considerable problem for the African retailer in expanding his business from the $28 a week level to the $70 a week level.

Unfortunately it is quite impossible to make any estimate as to how many of the 34,581 African retailers licensed in 1961 were in each of these two broad categories. A very extensive survey would be required to discover this. A great many African shops are in extremely remote areas. Impressions of the size of shops in each district formed by travelling along the roads and occasionally making short expeditions on foot to one or two villages are likely to be entirely misleading. The ratio of large to small shops varies greatly in different areas also, so that it would be very difficult to get an accurate picture by means of sampling.

THE RELATIONSHIP OF PRODUCE TRADING
TO DISTRIBUTIVE TRADING

The connection between produce trading and distributive trading in Tanganyika is extremely close. For many years the two types of trading were completely inseparable. In all levels the buying, marketing and exporting of produce was carried on by the same concerns which imported and distributed consumer goods. It is only in the last fifteen to twenty years that the two trades have begun to be at all separate.

Three things have tended to bring this about. One is the setting up of the producers co-operatives, which have taken a very large part of the produce trade out of the hands of the private dealers. The second is the considerable growth in the internal trade in locally grown foodstuffs between different parts of Tanganyika, and also between different parts of East Africa as a whole. The growth in this trade has made it necessary for quite a number of dealers to specialise entirely in this line of business, that is

in buying, selling and transporting produce up and down East
Africa. The business is so complex that it has become impossible to combine it successfully with dealing in other lines as
well. The third factor is the growth of the local milling industry: grain, rice and oilseeds of various sorts. Both milling
and produce trading require considerable amounts of capital.
The usual development has been for successful produce traders
to become millers. In doing so they carry on, or even expand,
their produce trading, but tend to give up any other, less profitable, lines of business - usually piecegoods - because they no
longer have the time or the necessary resources of management.

The position in 1961 was that the two main African-grown
cash crops, cotton and coffee, were marketed almost entirely
by the co-operatives, while most of the other African-grown
crops were marketed by produce dealers. In spite of the developments outlined above, the bulk of these minor cash crops
was handled by traders who are also, as wholesalers or retailers
distributors of consumer goods. In areas where a considerable
quantity of minor cash crops is produced, there are usually
several traders whose main business is produce dealing, but
who also do a sizable amount of wholesaling or retailing. This
is very much the case in the Southern Region, but also in the
Western and Central Regions. In other areas, where the amount
of minor cash crops produced is not large, the wholesalers and
retailers who deal in produce do so as only a minor part of their
businesses.

There is a variety of excellent reasons why produce trading
and distributive trading should be so closely linked in a country
like Tanganyika. Produce buying is naturally an extremely seasonal activity. If it is carried on by itself, the trader is either
almost totally inactive for more than half the year, incurring
considerable overheads while doing very little business, or he
has to close down altogether for part of the year and find alternative employment. The obvious solution is to turn to distributive
trading.

The quantity of produce to be bought in any one area is seldom
so great that the buyer is unable to carry on another business
at the same time. In this way he is able to make fuller use of
all his resources, his shop, his storage space, his staff, usually
himself, his wife and perhaps his children, his capital and his
transport. This last is of particular importance. Transport
costs are often an over-riding factor in produce trading. If a
two-way load can be obtained this is a very important consideration. A trader is much more likely to be able to arrange this if
he is a distributor as well as a produce buyer.

In a country where the growing of produce is scattered in small pockets over large areas, one of the essential require - ments for a successful buyer is to maintain a network of relia- ble agents in all the localities. The best way of doing this is to have agents who are permanently established in their respective localities. Almost the only means of doing this is for them to operate a small shop. There are three ways in which these small shopkeepers can be associated with the produce dealer. They can either be managers on a salary working directly for him, or they can be independent in name though obtain all their supplies on credit from him and sell all their purchases of pro- duce to him, or they can be independent in fact, having only an ad hoc trading arrangement with the dealer.

Another important advantage in combining produce buying and distributing is the additional facilities this provides for obtaining finance. Produce trading needs large amounts of working capital. The big produce dealer obtains this partly from the exporter, perhaps by selling forward or by means of a straight loan, or from the bank. As we proceed back along the chain of produce dealers and as they become smaller, so it becomes increasingly difficult and expensive for them to obtain the necessary finance. They may be able to obtain their working capital in the same way as the bigger dealers, but in smaller quantities. They may not, however, be able to obtain finance from the bank at all or to make arrangements for selling forward. In this case they are dependent on their own resources or on advances from the dealer to whom they sell. However, if they are distributing consumer goods, particularly piecegoods, they can normally obtain supplies of these on cre- dit, usually 90 days. As soon as the produce season begins they can sell many of these piecegoods, if necessary at cut prices, and so obtain increased working capital. This practice is very common, but cannot of course be used unless the trader combines distributing with produce buying.

In certain areas, particularly in the Southern Region, this practice is taken a stage further. Much of the crop is sold for- ward by the local buyers and the payment which they receive from the large dealers and exporters is partly in cash and partly in consumer goods, mainly piecegoods, which are used to stock up their shops ready for the first growers with money in their pockets from the sale of their produce. In this way the most rapid possible turnover is obtained.

This, of course, is another extremely important feature of combining distributive and produce trading. The fullest possible use is made of usually very limited capital resources, and the

rate of turnover is greatly increased, possibly almost doubled.
What could be more convenient for the customer or more desirable for the trader than that while the grower is having his
produce bought and weighed by the trader in front of the shop,
his wife is inside buying a new pair of khangas from the trader's
wife?

All these are quite sound and respectable economic reasons
for combining the two types of trade. As long as the trade is
truly competitive, both the grower and the consumer should
benefit from the factors listed above. They help the trader to
keep his costs down, thus enabling him to offer higher prices
to the growers, while at the same time selling consumer goods
more cheaply to consumers.

However, there are also a good many other less commendable
reasons for combining distribution and produce buying. The
practice enables the retailer-cum-produce-buyer to sell goods
on credit to growers against future delivery of crops. This in
itself is not necessarily undesirable, but the retailer normally
takes advantage of his position to obtain very favourable terms
for himself. In some areas buyers carry on a system of barter,
paying for the produce with consumer goods. This again usually
leads to abuses. Furthermore, the fact that the trader is both
buying produce and retailing gives him more room to manoeuvre
and to indulge in sharp practices. He can give the appearance
of making a generous offer on one half of the deal, while making
a very large profit out of the other half.

If a small retailer who buys produce is entirely dependent on
one dealer for his working capital and supplies of consumer good
then he in his turn is liable to be seriously exploited. It frequen
happens that the main produce dealer supplies the retailer with
goods on credit at a high price, he then buys produce back from
him at a correspondingly low price. The small retailer has littl
alternative but to accept this, as without the credit obtained in
this way he would be unable to carry on any produce buying at all
and probably only a reduced retail trade. If he tried to obtain
credit from another supplier with whom he had not previously
been dealing he would be unlikely to obtain better terms.

It should not be thought that these practices are universal, but
they are certainly very widespread.

We saw earlier that there are certain clear economic advantages in combining produce buying and distributive trading, and
these should be to the benefit of all concerned, whether growers,
consumers or traders. However, the system also unfortunately
facilitates certain undesirable practices; but it should be noted
that these malpractices are not a necessary part of the system,

but merely result from lack of commercial experience on the part of the growers on the one hand, and from the low level of commercial morality on the part of the traders on the other. It should also be noted that this low level of commercial morality is not confined to any one racial group.

Produce buying is on the whole a more risky business than wholesaling and retailing. Prices of most forms of produce fluctuate widely and frequently. However, profits are correspondingly greater. The existence of branch shops designed primarily for the purpose of buying produce is very strong circumstantial evidence of this. When produce buying is taken out of the hands of the dealers, it is no longer considered worth while to maintain these branches even though they may be doing a sizable retail business. It seems that the margin normally expected on produce trading at this level is about 10 per cent, while the wholesale margin on goods with a similarly rapid turnover is probably in the region of only 3 to 4 per cent.

4

THE FUNCTIONING OF THE DISTRIBUTION SYSTEM

MARGINS

The margins examined here are all gross margins, that is the difference between the cost of purchases and the value of sales. Transport charges are excluded as far as possible. The normal practice in England is to express the gross margin as a percentage of the selling price. Thus a margin of 20 per cent means that an article sold for $10 was bought by the trader for $8.

All the margins referred to in this survey are expressed as a percentage of the trader's cost of purchase. Thus if a trader buys an article for $8 and sells it for $10, the margin is cal - culated to be 25 per cent. This is the normal practice of wholesalers and retailers in Tanganyika. It is usual for the margins on consumer durables and capital goods, i.e. the agency lines handled mainly by the European-owned importing houses, to be expressed in the English way, as a percentage of the selling price. In this survey these figures have all been converted, and are expressed as a percentage of the cost price. Likewise, where comparisons are made with margins in England, the English margins have been converted to the same basis as the Tanganyika ones.

Before attempting an examination of the margins normally obtained by the main types of traders, it is necessary to under - stand something of the pricing policies which prevail in Tangan - yika, as well as something of the factors which affect the size of gross margins.

In England prices of goods are determined in three ways. The price may be fixed by the manufacturer under the system known as resale price maintenance; it may be suggested by the manufacturer, who publishes a recommended retail price; and, finally, it can be determined solely by the retailer. Resale price maintenance is believed to cover just under one half of all the retail sales made in the United Kingdom. Some years ago it covered more than this, but the spread of supermarkets and discount stores has reduced its prevalence. Nevertheless more or less uniform prices are charged in outlets of the same

type throughout the United Kingdom. It is the rule in all types
of store (excluding those dealing with antiques or second-hand
goods) for prices to be fixed and there is no question of bargaining between retailer and customer. If the customer con-
siders the price too high he goes elsewhere.

It would be hard to imagine a greater contrast to the situation which prevails in Tanganyika. There is no legally enforce-
able resale price maintenance in Tanganyika, and the practice
is almost, though not completely, unknown. The two most outstanding examples of it are provided by the pricing of cigarettes,
where there is virtually only one supplier, and of petrol, where
there is only a small number of suppliers, who are able to reach
an agreement as to prices charged at the pump. Cigarettes also
provide about the only example of a uniform price for one commodity throughout the country.   Prices for petrol are uniform
in each area, but they differ in various parts of the country
according to the distance from the port of entry into East Africa.

In the case of other goods, fixed prices are very much the
exception, outside a few European-owned retail stores and a
very few Asian-owned stores, mostly catering for European customers; prices are arrived at only after a process of bargaining.
The only exceptions to this are the daily-consumed foodstuffs
and provisions. In each area there are conventionally accepted
retail prices of these items, such as sugar, rice, maize meal,
tinned milk, soap, etc. However, these prices are not uniform
throughout the country; they differ from area to area, and they
also vary from time to time if the wholesale price fluctuates
beyond certain limits.

While convention is an all-important factor in deciding the
retail price of goods in England, it plays a comparatively small
part in Tanganyika. There are few conventional prices. The
price is arrived at in the light of the circumstances prevailing
at the time of each transaction.

The price arrived at as a result of the usual bargaining is
determined by the interplay of various factors: the supply and
demand position of the particular goods in the area concerned;
the customer's knowledge of the quality and the actual cost price
of the goods he requires; whether purchases of other goods,
with possibly higher margins, are being made at the same time;
whether the sale is for cash or on credit; whether the retailer
is in urgent need of cash to meet demands from his suppliers
or possibly to use for produce buying; or, finally, the degree
of urgency with which the customer requires the article concerned.
For example, it will be found that when the baby starts crying
late in the evening, the rubber teat for the feeding bottle has been

mislaid and only one shop stocking rubber teats is open, then
the price demanded will be 35 cents, though next morning it
will have fallen to only 10 cents. In the same way if there is
only one motor spares dealer in a district, a part is broken,
an urgent journey has to be made and the lorry-owner does not
know the cost price of the part, then a margin of 1, 000 per cent
may well be charged. It must be emphasised, however, that
margins of this sort are exceptional; most prudent parents,
after all, keep a spare rubber teat somewhere in the house.

At the various wholesaling levels, i. e. between importer
and wholesaler, wholesaler and sub-wholesaler and sub-wholesaler and retailer, similar considerations apply when reaching
agreement on a price, though other factors also have to be
considered here.

Only importers with agency lines are able to do a wholesale
business on the basis of anything like fixed prices and fixed
terms, and even then it is seldom possible to stick to these
rigidly. Most agency lines, once they have passed from the
hands of the importers into those of the wholesalers or sub-
wholesalers, are as much the subject of bargaining as any other
lines. The element of bargaining is introduced in connection
with bulk discounts, credit terms etc. Again cigarettes are
about the only important exception to this.

It has to be remembered that each transaction which takes
place between two traders, for instance between a wholesaler
and a sub-wholesaler or a retailer, is an individual transaction
to be negotiated on the basis of the conditions prevailing at the
time. Comparatively few permanent business relationships
are built up. It is very seldom possible to place an order as
part of a regular series and know that the terms obtained will
be the same, or differ only in one or two minor respects, from
the terms obtained on previous orders placed with the same
supplier. Factors which would be taken for granted if a continuous business relationship based on trust had been built up
have to be considered afresh and are the subject of detailed
bargaining on each occasion.

As the whole basis of the bargaining is the price to be paid,
all the other factors have to be taken into account before the
price can be settled.

The supply and demand position naturally is a fundamental
consideration. There can be big fluctuations in supplies and in
demand for almost all types of goods. This is because dis -
tances over which supplies have to come are great, and a hold-
up can easily occur. Supplies of local foodstuffs in particular
can fluctuate sharply, while the market is small and also liable

to abrupt changes, for seasonal or other reasons.

The wholesaler can find himself overstocked and short of ready cash, with suppliers pressing for payment. He may wish to raise cash in order to do some produce buying. For either of these reasons he may be anxious to make a sale and cut his price accordingly. He may, of course, have information that other traders are overstocked and likely to depress the market, or that the price of supplies is likely to fall for some other reason. This may make him eager to sell.

On the other hand, the buyer may be particularly anxious to increase his stocks, possibly at the beginning of the season or, if of piecegoods, before a holiday such as Id el Fitr or Easter, when good business is done. He may, therefore, be prepared to pay high prices. He may also be particularly anxious to obtain supplies on credit. It is very seldom that any specific charge for credit is laid down by the wholesaler. The cost is incorporated in the price and is the subject of bargaining. A large regular customer who is a good risk naturally obtains a very much better price than a small, occasional customer whose credit-rating is low. However, if the large customer is known to be in urgent need of credit, naturally the price he has to pay for his supplies will be considerably higher. If the small customer needs credit badly, he is likely to have to pay very high prices indeed for his supplies.

On a large order it is possible that part will be obtained for cash, the rest for vaying period of credit, 30, 60, 90 or possibly 120 days. The prices of the slow-moving lines bought on the longer credit terms are likely to be high.

The prices asked for the first items of a small retailer's order are usually kept very low, but for the later items they tend to rise. As prices are practically never written up for buyers to see, it is not possible to attract customers into the shop by displaying loss leaders; but it is very common, in fact almost standard practice, for fast-moving bulk purchases to be sold at cut-throat prices, while the prices of slow-moving lines are greatly increased. This takes place at the wholesale as well as the retail level.

At the retail level the prices of khangas vary according to the popularity of the colour and design, even though the quality is identical. This is also taken back to the wholesale level, particularly with cotton or rayon printed materials. The same design is usually sold in sets of about five different colours. Almost always one colour sells very much better than the rest, in which case its price is normally increased by anything up to 50 per cent above the others.

Prices also vary very much according to the size of the order. Piecegoods can be sold in wholesale quantities varying from a 15-yard length to a bale of perhaps 1,000 yards or more. Naturally the difference in the price per yard between the two orders will be very considerable.

These are some of the main factors which have to be taken into consideration when a price is agreed between two traders. It will be seen from this that any idea of there being a recognised or normal price level for particular goods is in most cases quite unrealistic. This in turn means that there is seldom a normal or typical margin applied by traders to the various types of good at different levels of the distribution network. Conditions vary enormously between transactions, and these variations all tend to be reflected in changes in the size of the margin.

A further complicating factor is the very large fluctuations which take place in the cost price of most goods distributed in Tanganyika. This means that it is seldom possible to maintain a fixed margin. Few traders can think in terms of selling at cost plus x per cent. The size of the margin is determined by the cost of supplies on the one hand and the state of the market on the other. As both of these vary greatly, the size of the margin necessarily varies considerably also.

The frequent and considerable fluctuations in the price of so many goods is the result of various factors. Both the supply and demand for many items is highly seasonal. The market is small, distances are great and communications are often tenuous. This means that local shortages and surpluses frequently develop. The same is to a great extent true of imported supplies also. The Tanganyika market for most goods is a small one and source of supply are distant. Prices in small export markets such as Tanganyika tend to fluctuate more than in the large home market as manufacturers normally try to keep prices in large markets as steady as possible. This means that temporary shortages and surpluses in world supplies are reflected in sharp price movements in small markets like Tanganyika.

From all this it is clear that it would be misleading in most cases to make a list of the normal margins obtained on the different types of goods distributed in Tanganyika. However, even if this is misleading, it should be possible to average gross margins for different types of traders. Over the course of a year and dealing in a wide variety of lines, as most traders do, margins must tend to average out, so that it should be realistic to say what average gross margins traders in a particular line of business do obtain. Here again, however, there are problems largely centring on the phrase "a particular line of business".

The gross margins of traders vary so enormously according to their particular circumstances.

For these reasons, any broad generalisations about gross margins by main types of traders would be extremely misleading. It is necessary to examine particular circumstances in considerable detail. The extent of the detail can be gauged from the following list of factors which affect the average gross margins of traders.

The general line of goods dealt in clearly is important, and also the stage of the distributive process at which the trader operates, whether importer, wholesaler, sub-wholesaler or retailer. But here we at once run into immense difficulties. We have seen that very few traders specialise in only one line of business. Even more significant, as far as the size of gross margins is concerned, is whether a trader concentrates on fast-moving bulk lines, or slow-moving, perhaps even luxury or semi-luxury lines. The varying proportions of the different types of goods have a considerable effect on the size of margins. Furthermore, we have seen that in almost all cases importers, wholesalers and sub-wholesalers each engage in all the stages subsequent to their own in the distribution process. The proportion of their trade which is conducted at each stage naturally affects their gross margins.

In addition to these considerations, the area in which the trader operates has an important influence on the size of his gross margin. There are two reasons for this. In an urban area, or other areas where the level of demand is high, sales naturally tend to be very much greater than in a rural area with a low level of demand. The turnover of stocks is very much more rapid. In an urban area it may be possible to turn over stocks worth say $700 as often as once a week, while in a rural area it might take three months to sell this amount. Clearly the trader who is selling $700 worth of goods every week is able to operate on a very much lower margin than the trader who can only do this amount of business in three months. The second reason is that a business can be run on very much smaller stocks in an accessible urban area than in a distant rural location. This is because it is possible to obtain supplies regularly, at no great expense and at frequent intervals from a wholesaler located conveniently nearby.

An extreme example of this is provided by a small general provisions retailer in Dar es Salaam who can obtain a sack of sugar, rice, etc., from the wholesaler every day if necessary, delivered to his shop at no extra cost, or at the most for the cost of 14 cents a bag. In a remote area, even if the rate of

turnover is as high as that of the shop in Dar es Salaam, it is
frequently necessary, if transport costs are not going to be
prohibitive, to wait until a lorry-load can be bought, perhaps
once or at the most twice a month. This means that, for a
trader of this size, a great deal of capital has to be tied up in
stocks, even of the fast-moving lines.

Margins on fast and slow-moving lines

The most striking feature of the margins obtained by trader
in Tanganyika is the enormous difference between the margins
charged on the bulk, fast-moving lines and the margins charge
on the slower-moving lines in any particular trade. As an
example of this, the average margin between duty paid landed
cost and the retail price of black material for kanikis is betwe
20 and 25 per cent, except in very remote areas, while for
khangas it normally varies between 20 and 33 per cent, though
exceptionally popular designs will show a larger mark-up. On
the other hand the average margin between imported price and
retail on printed spun rayon dress materials is about 75 per
cent. Sometimes it may be down to 33 per cent and sometimes
it may go up to 100 or 125 per cent, but 75 per cent is about
the average.

The margin on the most popular make of ready-made shirts
from Hong Kong, which easily outsells all other brands, is nor
mally only 30 per cent, while on other types of shirts it is
usually 60 to 75 per cent. It is interesting to note that in Engl
the gross margins for both men's and women's wear from the
manufacturer to the consumer average 50 per cent. This cove
a variation normally between about 35 per cent on fast-moving
lines and about 66 per cent on the more expensive slow-moving
lines.

In foodstuffs and provisions there is an equally large gulf be
tween the fast and slow-moving lines in Tanganyika. The bulk
foodstuffs are generally distributed from the big produce deale
or the miller to the consumer on very low margins, except in
times of shortage, when margins increase considerably. On
imported goods, the margins between the imported price and
the retail price in the main centres of consumption for such
fast-moving lines as the popular brands of tinned milk or ghee
substitute are between 25 and 30 per cent. But the margins
on the slow-moving lines are very generous. On such items as
tinned pears, jam or imported dates, for which there is no ma
market, gross margins vary between 50 and 75 per cent and fo
many items are even more.

In building materials we come across the same pattern. Cer
and corrugated iron sheets are distributed for a total gross ma

of between 20 and 33 per cent, but most of the slow-moving builders' supplies are distributed on a gross margin of 60 to 100 per cent.

What are the reasons for this sharp contrast in the margins on fast and slow-moving lines?   In the first place, a very large part of turnover in Tanganyika is concentrated in a very small range of goods - very much more so than in England. In many parts of Tanganyika sales of americani and black material together form half of the total value of sales in the piecegoods trade; in most rural areas they form between a quarter and a third of the total. In England there are no two lines which form anything like this proportion of total sales. Similarly in foodstuffs and provisions, a very small selection of commodities constitutes an overwhelming proportion of total sales.

In the second place conditions in Tanganyika are extremely competitive. There are a great many small wholesalers and retailers, but the competition is heavily concentrated on the fast-moving lines. Except in the large centres, where it is possible for some traders to specialise in the slow-moving lines, every trader has to stock the fast-moving lines if he is to do any business at all. Competition, therefore, in these lines is intense. Furthermore everybody knows the quality and the price of these standard lines; thus it is impossible to increase the margins by exploiting the ignorance of the customers.

These factors account for the very low prices of the bulk lines. Other factors account for the high prices of the slow-moving lines. Many of the slow-moving lines are very slow-moving indeed, because the market in Tanganyika is in any case small and because such a large part of it is accounted for by the bulk lines. In many lines, and in most areas, the sales are so small that there is only room for one or two dealers in any special line. Hence the competition is very much less keen than in bulk lines. There are various trades which are obvious examples of this, chemists' and photographic goods, the more expensive clothing and even builders' and decorators' supplies. There are very few centres outside Dar es Salaam that have a big enough trade to support more than a handful of traders in these lines, sometimes only one. Since these are not standard lines, and since there is an enormous variety of qualities and prices, the customer is much less likely to know the true cost of the article he is buying. He usually makes purchases of this type of goods very infrequently. He is, therefore, much more likely to be confused over quality and price, and the trader is much more likely to be able to make a "fortuitous" profit.

In these circumstances the very real advantage of success -
fully establishing a brand name can be seen very clearly. In
this respect it is interesting to note the dominant position which
one or two brands have been able to attain in several lines.
Certain brands of ready-made shirts, watches and bicycles
immediately come to mind. The margin on the brands concerned is very much less than on unbranded goods or goods
with a poorly known brand name. The reason for this is partly
that their turnover is greater, more shops stock them and the
competition is therefore greater, but it is mainly because the
brand name really is some guarantee of quality to the consumer
He knows exactly what he is buying for once, and he knows what
its price should be. Therefore, if he sticks to the well-known
brands, he will almost invariably be getting better value for
his money. This clearly demonstrates the big advantage a
well-known branded product has in a market where there are
few branded goods, and where quality and price can be such a
hit-or-miss affair for the average consumer.

These considerations apply mainly at the retail level, but it
frequently happens that the small retailer is in the same position when buying from a wholesaler. He too is ignorant of the
quality and true cost. At the wholesale level there is less
likelihood of these "fortuitous" profits, but traders obviously
are aware that it is possible to obtain wide margins on many
slow-moving lines. Therefore, since margins are so tight on
the fast-moving lines, they naturally tend to compensate for
this by obtaining higher margins on the slow-moving lines.

Because of this wide divergence in margins between bulk
lines and slow-moving lines, it is very difficult to make any
generalisations about the average size of margins. However,
most traders do much of their business in the fast-moving bulk
lines, on which the margins are low. This must necessarily
be so. Thus, even though margins on certain items may be
very high, overall gross margins are not greatly raised, since
the high-margin lines usually form only a small part of total
turnover. There are of course exceptions to this, and some
traders may be fortunate enough to do a sizable part of their
business in the more profitable lines. A very few specialise
in the slow-moving lines and their gross margins are usually
very high. Nevertheless it must be remembered that the turnover in these lines is usually not very large, a big investment
in stocks has to be made, and a greater risk has to be run as
a result of such factors as changes in fashion and sharp changes
in supply and demand.

This wide variation in margins extends right down to the

level of the small general store. In Dar es Salaam, for instance,
the retailer's margin on such items as sugar, rice, salt, tinned
milk, cigarettes etc., varies from only 5 per cent to about 12
per cent. But his margin on a comparatively slow-moving line
like dates or dagaa is about 33 per cent, while on such items
as sewing thread, sweets or writing paper it may be 50 to 100
per cent.

Variations according to locality

Another outstanding feature is the wide variation between the
margins obtained by traders in the same line of business in different localities. This is most easily examined at the level of
the small general provision store, as these are universal
throughout Tanganyika and are dealing in broadly the same type
of goods. It is also possible to obtain more accurate information about their average gross margins, since the price of most
of the goods they sell is not a question of bargaining, but is
controlled by local convention.

The average gross margin of a fairly large general provision store, usually owned by an Arab, in the African part of
Dar es Salaam with a turnover of about $14,000 a year, is about
$12\frac{1}{2}$ per cent. A similar margin is obtained by the same sort
of general store in the centre of any of the larger towns, say
Tanga, Moshi or Mwanza. For a smaller African-owned general store on the outskirts of Dar es Salaam, doing perhaps between $2,800 and $5,600 worth of business a year, the average
gross margin is about 15 per cent.

An Arab or Asian-owned shop in one of the lesser towns
such as Shinyanga or Korogwe, with a turnover of around
$8,400 to $14,000, obtains a gross margin of between 15 and
18 per cent; while the gross margin of a small African-owned
shop on the edge of the township area of either Bukoba or Mwanza
is between 22 and 25 per cent. For a store with a rather larger
turnover outside Mwanza town, but in the same district, and
stocking a rather wider range of goods than the average, many
items being in the rather more expensive slow-moving lines,
the average gross margin is about 33 per cent.   But a store
of this type is not strictly comparable with the others.

A small general food and provisions shop at a good distance
from any sizable centre normally obtains a margin of about
25 to 30 per cent. In very remote areas this may rise to 35
per cent and possibly more, but this wide margin is only obtained if the retailer can buy direct from a wholesaler.   Normally he will have to accept a smaller margin than this and
buy from a sub-wholesaler.

From this it will be seen that there is again a very big

divergence between the margin obtained, on the one hand, by a
general provisions store in a large centre with a fair-sized
turnover and able to get supplies at short notice without transport problems and on the other hand, a similar, though much
smaller shop, in a rural area where these conditions do not
apply. In a really remote area the margin can be three times
that obtained in an urban centre and this, it must be remembered, is excluding transport costs. Prices in remote areas
are always very much higher than in the main centres. This
is only to be expected, as the retailers in these areas have
many difficulties, while their turnover is often so small that,
if their margins were less, they would barely be able to make
a living of any sort out of their shops. As it is, many shops
are open part-time and are run in conjunction with some other
activity, usually farming.

As a basis for comparison it is interesting to note that the
gross margin for grocers and provision dealers in the United
Kingdom in 1957 was 18 per cent. Thus the general provisions
dealers in the main centres in Tanganyika compare very favour
ably as far as margins are concerned. It must be remembered
though, that the standard of premises, service, display, pack-
aging etc., is very much higher in England than in Tanganyika,
although English grocers usually have a considerably larger
turnover to help cover the cost of these additional overheads.

General Stores

The shops we have been considering so far have been those
dealing solely in foodstuffs and provisions. If we turn to those
general stores, common all over Tanganyika, dealing not only
in these lines, but also in piecegoods and sundries of all sorts,
we run into much greater difficulties in making comparisons of
margins. For one thing the relative importance of the different
lines affects the gross margin considerably, in particular, what
proportion of the piecegoods are bulk lines and what proportion
fancy goods. The other main problem is that most of the non-
provisions items do not have a conventional price but are the
subject of bargaining. Thus it is extremely difficult to obtain
reliable retail prices for many of the goods sold. As an example of this problem, on several occasions during this enquiry,
retailers stated their average selling price for various items.
During the interviews customers came in to bargain for the
goods concerned. The final selling price was almost invariably
above the average price quoted by the retailer. The retailers in
question were unaware at the time that the bargaining was being
followed.

Variations in the sources of supply and the amount of credit received are further complicating factors. In Tabora, for instance, two small shops, selling mainly piecegoods and with similar stock, had completely different average gross margins. One retailer bought most of his supplies from local wholesalers on 30 days credit and naturally his overall gross margin was low, in the region of $7\frac{1}{2}$ per cent to 10 per cent. The retailer next door bought most of his supplies from wholesalers in Dar es Salaam and mainly paid cash. His overall gross margin appeared to be at least 15 per cent.

In spite of these difficulties some generalisations can be made, though they must be treated with due caution. In the main centres small retail shops selling piecegoods tend to specialise in piecegoods only, often employing one or more tailors. They seldom deal in provisions as well. With a turn-over of between $5,600 and $11,200, mostly in the cheaper goods for the African market on which margins are low, these retailers have an average gross margin of 12-17 per cent, the higher margin being mostly for those who also employ a tailor. The normal practice is for the shopkeeper to own the sewing machine and for the charge for making-up to be split 50-50 between tailor and shopkeeper. In some areas a price is quoted to the customer for the garment complete and the tailor is paid a fixed rate by the shopkeeper. The charge to the cus-tomer for making-up a pair of shorts varies between 21 cents and 42 cents according to the quality of the work, and whether it is done in a rural area or in a town. The charge for making-up a dress varies between about 42 cents and 84 cents.

In the main centres there are usually some shops which specialise in rather higher-quality piecegoods and fancy goods, mainly for the African market, but also to some extent for the Asian market. The turnover of these shops is often rather more than that of the small retailer catering for the normal African trade, perhaps $11,200 to $22,400. The overall gross margin of these traders will be considerably higher also, any-thing from 25 to 35 per cent. This trade requires more know-ledge, a bigger stock and is more affected by the vagaries of fashion.

Outside the main towns there are scarcely any traders who specialise only in piecegoods. Almost all combine foodstuffs, provisions, piecegoods and sundries. In a fairly well-frequented trading centre the average gross margin of a general retail store of this type is about 25 per cent. But a complicating fac-tor here is that this type of trader is frequently engaged in sub-wholesaling, and while this will raise his total sales it is likely to bring down his overall gross margin. In the more distant trading centres and minor settlements the overall gross margin probably rises to 30 to 35 per cent.

Comparisons of the gross margins of this type of shop with its equivalent in the United Kingdom cannot be made very satisfactorily, as there are few if any shops in the United Kingdom stocking the same range of goods. However, if we take women' wear shops as being the nearest equivalent in the piecegoods field, we find that their average gross margin in 1957 came to 38 per cent, but a very high proportion of their supplies was obtained direct from the manufacturers, so that this figure covers both the wholesale and retail margin for much of the trade. The wholesaler's margin on piecegoods in the United Kingdom was 15 per cent, so that the margin in respect of the retail side alone was about 23 to 25 per cent. This clearly indicates that the average margins charged by retailers in Tanganyika, in the towns at any rate, are very competitive. In the more remote areas margins are undoubtedly less competitive, though this is in most cases justified by the very much smaller turnover and the difficulties of obtaining supplies and of maintaining larger stocks.

Various specialist retailers

Turning to some of the more specialist retailers, we find in the building materials trade, for instance, that the gross margin is very much affected by the proportion of the total turnover which is in cement and C.I. sheets, whether large stocks of these have to be held, or whether it is possible to order supplies quickly from Dar es Salaam. Some dealers make most of their sales to big customers such as building contractors, local authorities and missions, giving bulk discounts; others do more of their trade with small customers, mostly small builders. Only in the main centres is there a big enough demand for builders' supplies to justify the existence of more than two or three traders in this line. In places of the size of Dodoma or Musoma, for instance, there are usually two or three traders in building materials, and one of these probably does most of the business. This means that, though the competition in the bulk lines is usually intense - firms other than building materials specialists often trade in these lines as well - competition in the slow-moving items is frequently minimal, and margins are high.

A big building materials dealer in one of the larger centres with a turnover in the range of $140,000 to $280,000 a year, over half of which is in the bulk lines, probably obtains a gross margin of about 15 per cent. A smaller dealer in a minor centre, possibly doing less business in the bulk lines, often obtains a very much higher gross margin.

In the United Kingdom the gross margin obtained by whole-salers, not retailers, of building materials, fitments and decorators' supplies was 23 per cent in 1950. The gross margin in the ironmongery and hardware trade in 1957 was 37 per cent. There are probably not many dealers in Tanganyika who obtain overall gross margins higher than these. We have here a striking example of the contrast in margins between fast and slow-moving lines in Tanganyika. The margins on cement and C.I. sheets are very low, often not more that 6 or 7 per cent, but the margins on the various fittings etc., are by contrast exorbitant, often 100 per cent or more. Nevertheless, the overall gross margin is not excessive, since the bulk lines reduce it very sharply. In the United Kingdom the spread of margins between fast and slow-moving lines is not as great, and the prices charged for slow-moving items are not as exorbitant as they frequently are in Tanganyika, but the overall gross margins in England are probably no lower, and in many cases higher, though it should be remembered that the variety of stock carried is usually greater, and delays in delivery are less.

The margins obtained by traders specialising in groceries, provisions and sundries for the European market are normally high. In some of the more remote centres they can be very high indeed. The retail margin on the normal range of tinned goods and preserves is about 20 per cent, but this is of course on top of a price already increased by quite heavy transport charges and import duties. Many lines are imported direct, including cosmetics, and the margins on these are never less than 50 per cent and may be up to 100 per cent. Sundry items such as glassware, toys etc., almost all have a mark-up of 100 per cent, but very few retailers stock these lines. The average gross margin in this trade is probably between 30 and 40 per cent. In the United Kingdom the average gross margin for grocers and provision dealers was 18 per cent, and for toiletries, 33 per cent.

There are very few chemists shops in Tanganyika outside Dar es Salaam, and in most places where such a shop exists it is the only one. The margin on the usual lines of toilet articles and patent medicines is between 30 and 50 per cent, but on most drugs the standard margin seems to be 100 per cent.

The margins on clothes, mainly for the European market, are also very high. The overall gross margin is normally 50 to 60 per cent, and for many items it can be as high as 100

per cent. Outside Dar es Salaam the trade of these shops, and
of the European-style grocers, has been falling very rapidly re
cently as the number of European customers decreases.

Wholesale margins

In the wholesale trade we are faced with an even greater
variety of conditions and individual circumstances than in the
retail trade, so that generalisations are even more difficult to
make and more liable to be misleading. This unfortunately
means that almost all statements have to be hedged with a variety of provisos, which is unsatisfactory, but unavoidable.

Starting with the wholesalers in Dar es Salaam who are
mainly supplying the African market we again find the extreme
contrast between the margins on the fast and the slow-moving
lines. In piecegoods, the average margins obtained by the big
importer/wholesalers on the bulk lines such as americani,
black material and khangas is only 2 to 3 per cent, but on
fancy lines it is 10 to 12 per cent, and can occasionally go up
to 15 per cent. On cheap ready-made clothing the wholesale
margin is 10 to 15 per cent, and on some lines, for instance
second-hand clothing, can rise to 20 per cent. The average
gross margin of a big wholesaler who concentrates on the bulk
lines was, in 1961, 3 to 4 per cent. For a wholesaler who did
most of his business in the more fancy lines it was 7 to 10 per
cent, and for the few who specialised in cheap clothing it was
about 12 to 15 per cent.

In the United Kingdom the wholesale margin on piecegoods
and dress materials was 13 per cent in 1950 and on clothing
$16\frac{1}{2}$ per cent. Thus, purely on a comparison of margins, Dar
es Salaam wholesalers show up very well.

In the wholesale trade in foodstuffs and provisions the margins are equally low on the bulk lines, again only 2 to 3 per
cent - and sometimes as little as 1 per cent. For other produce lines, such as peas and beans the average margin is
about 8 to 10 per cent, while on provisions such as tinned
milk, ghee, matches etc., which are imported direct from
abroad, the margin is between 8 and 12 per cent. On such
imported lines as spices, ginger or dates the importer/
wholesaler's margin is about 12 to 18 per cent.

The average gross margin of a large foodstuffs and provisions wholesaler doing a good trade in the bulk lines is 5 to 6
per cent. If the wholesaler specialises in the imported provisions lines his gross margin may average 10 to 12 per cent.
Margins somewhere between these figures are obtained by
most provisions wholesalers, in accordance with the proportion of each type of business which they conduct.

Wholesalers, whether in Dar es Salaam or in towns up-country, who buy their supplies of bulk food and provisions lines from importers or big produce dealers work on very small margins for these lines, normally only 3 to 4 per cent. This is very often merely the size of the discount which they receive from the importing firms for buying in bulk quantities. The margin on the fast-moving foodstuffs bought from the big provision dealers and sold by these wholesalers by the bag to the local retailers is normally only 2 to 3 per cent.   This section of the trade is probably the most competitive in the whole distribution system. It should be noted also that most of the complaints about incorrect weights are levelled at this section of the trade. Complaints are very seldom made against the large dealers, who in any case are mostly selling to wholesalers who carefully weigh the goods they receive. The complaints are by the retailers against the wholesalers.

The frequency with which short weights are given by whole-salers in the foodstuffs trade means that actual gross margins are often more than apparent gross margins, and this may make a difference of 2 to 3 per cent, though seldom more. (See also below, page 148.)

Most wholesalers in this section of the trade deal in sundry provisions as well as foodstuffs and the margins on these are invariably greater than on the foodstuffs. The average gross margin obtained on these sundry provisions is about 8 to 10 per cent, so that the overall gross margin for a wholesaler of this type is usually between 5 and 7 per cent. However, it is not possible to be at all specific about this, since there is yet another important factor which affects the size of whole-salers' margins. This is the problem of the amount of credit given and received, and at what effective rates.

We have already seen that there is seldom a standard charge for credit, or to put it another way, there is seldom a standard discount for cash. Some of the larger importers give more or less standard cash discounts on certain lines, but wholesalers practically never give a standard discount, though naturally there is a fairly well-recognised scale of charges for credit in most trades. However, as one proceeds further down the chain of distributors, the variations in the charges for credit become bigger, as, of course, do the charges themselves. This is because the smaller the trader, the bigger is likely to be the variation in the individual cir-cumstances, both as between one trader and another, and as between one transaction and another. The smaller the tra-ders are, the greater become the "imperfections" in the supply of credit, and the greater also becomes the degree of risk involved.

For the wholesalers in the main centres the cost of 90 days credit is normally an increase of $2\frac{1}{2}$ to 3 per cent in the price of purchases, while their customers normally have to pay them an extra 5 per cent for 90 days credit. Thus the giving of cre - dit can increase the wholesaler's margin by 2 to $2\frac{1}{2}$ per cent. If he obtains finance from his bank, the increase will be a frac- tion more. However, it is unlikely to increase his overall gross margin by as much as 2 per cent, since very few whole- salers in 1961 did the whole of their business on credit. This is particularly true of the foodstuffs and provisions trade, where an increasing proportion of the business is done for cash. The bulk supplies, on which the margins are so low and which turn over rapidly, are normally bought and sold for cash, though short-term credit, of perhaps 30 days, is often given, and the charge for this is naturally less. On the other hand the few wholesalers who are in a very strong financial posi - tion and able to buy all or most of their supplies for cash and to sell on credit are naturally able to increase their overall gross margins considerably, by as much as 4 or 5 per cent, but there are few in a position to do this.

Between sub-wholesalers and retailers the charge for cre- dit can, and usually does, rise considerably above 5 per cent, though here again the charge on the bulk lines is lower and the period of credit usually shorter also. It is on the fancy goods sold by sub-wholesalers to retailers, often on open credit, that the difference between cash and credit prices can often be as much as 15 per cent, sometimes more.

A wholesaler dealing mainly in piecegoods in one of the main up-country centres probably obtains an overall gross margin of somewhere between 6 and 12 per cent, varying according to the different circumstances enumerated above. As a very rough guide, he would normally expect to obtain $2\frac{1}{2}$ to 3 per cent on the bulk lines, 10 to 12 per cent on the non- standard lines, and for a very few lines up to 20 per cent.

In a small town or trading centre, slightly more off the main routes, such as perhaps Tukuyu, Masasi or Singida, a piecegoods wholesaler obtains a gross margin of something more like 10 to 15 per cent. Again of course his turnover is likely to be smaller than that of a wholesaler in a main centre.

When we come to the problem of the gross margin obtained by sub-wholesalers, who normally deal in the whole range of goods for the African market, it is practically impossible to sort out the gross margins obtained on the two parts of the

business, the retailing side and the sub-wholesaling side. Also
the variations in the margins obtained in different circumstances are enormous. In general it can be said that at this
stage also the margins on the fast-moving lines are low,   5 per
cent and seldom more than 10 per cent, except in times of
shortage. But on the non-standard or fancy lines the margins
rise steeply as we have seen, often helped by a steep charge
for credit. It should also be remembered that the turnover of
these lines at this level in the distribution system is very
small.

We have already mentioned that there are a great many
small importer/wholesalers in Dar es Salaam dealing in sundry goods and various specialised lines on which the margins
tend to be very much above the average. On such items as
household linen, i.e. bedspreads or towels, these wholesalers
obtain a margin of 15 to 25 per cent, sometimes as much as
30 per cent, on travel goods and alarm clocks between 30 and
40 per cent. These are wholesale margins, though it is true
that very few orders are for more than 6 or 12 of any one item
at a time. Clearly margins of this sort are not competitive
with the margins charged by large sundries dealers in Mombasa.

The subject of margins is an extremely complex one, and it
cannot be dealt with satisfactorily as only one subject out of
several in a study of this length. Typical margins, hedged by
a great many provisos, have been given for the main types of
traders. The margins on individual items have scarcely been
touched upon. In order to give a true and realistic picture of
these, a full-scale survey on this subject alone would have to
be launched, and the problems to be solved, both in obtaining
accurate and representative information and in analysing it,
would be immense. Nothing has been said in this section about
the margins on capital goods or consumer durables. The variations in this field are so great that anything short of a detailed analysis seems valueless. In very broad terms, the
overall gross margin on the items in this class which might
be described as being of medium cost is about 25 to 33 per
cent. On very large items the margin is only 10 per cent.
Many capital goods items are handled by manufacturers' representatives, whose margins are normally between 5 and 10 per
cent - for certain non-technical items, less.

Overall gross margins in Tanganyika

The purpose of this section has been to examine the overall
structure of margins in the various main sectors of trade in
Tanganyika. On the basis of this examination various comments can be made.

The <u>overall</u> gross margins obtained by traders in Tangan -
yika are not high. Considering the difficulties of distribution
in the conditions prevailing in Tanganyika, i.e. problems of
distances, small markets, seasonal variations etc., the
average costs of distribution are low.

This finding does not accord with the general view held by
the public. There are several explanations of this. The main
reasons for the low average cost of distribution are the low
margins charged on the bulk items distributed which form a
high proportion of the total trade, and the low level of income
earned by most traders. The public takes the price of these
goods for granted, and is not generally aware of the very low
margins that traders obtain on them. People only become
aware of the prices of these goods and the margins obtained on
them in times of shortage, when both rise rapidly, and the
public feels it is being exploited - which sometimes it is.

The margins on the slow-moving lines, the fancy lines, the
occasional purchases for most people, are very high. The
average Tanganyikan is well aware of this. He is also aware
that he almost always has to bargain for these items and that
prices vary enormously from place to place, from month to
month and from individual to individual. The public, not un-
naturally, feels that it is being exploited and that, to put it
bluntly, the traders are operating a racket. There is a tendency to forget that day-to-day requirements are supplied at
very low prices indeed. Furthermore, those members of the
public who are most aware of pricing problems, and are the
most vocal about them, are precisely those who buy least of
the bulk lines and most of the high-cost, slow-moving lines.
They suffer most from the structure of prices now operating
in Tanganyika.

When accusations are made of excessive margins and pro-
fiteering, it is possible to point to whole sections of the distribution system where high margins undeniably exist, for
instance, chemists' and photographic goods, motor spares,
and European-style clothing or household goods. The turnover
in these lines forms only a fraction of the total, but this is
seldom remembered.

A further reason why it is generally believed that margins
are excessive in Tanganyika is the memory of the situation
existing some years ago. In the postwar years, when there
were serious shortages of most goods, fewer traders and
much less competition, margins were undoubtedly very high,
and profits often very great. But these conditions disappeared
some time ago. During the last three years or so, margins in

most lines have undoubtedly been squeezed still further. Total
sales have not been rising, but the number of traders has increased, particularly in the main centres. More important,
the days of really lavish credit are over. Traders have now
to watch their margins much more carefully, trying to obtain
a more rapid turnover with lower margins. Margins in 1961
were undoubtedly much slimmer than they had been three or
four years before. This narrowing of margins does not seem
to be a temporary phenomenon. It is generally realised that
the volume of credit given three or four years ago was excessive, and those who supply the credit have no intention of re-
turning to the conditions of those years.

STOCKS AND SEASONAL FACTORS

In the course of a survey of this kind, in which a sample
of traders of various types in many parts of the country was
interviewed, information can be obtained on the size of stocks
held by traders of different types in different lines of business,
but it is not possible to make any estimates of the total value
of the stocks held by different types of traders in the whole of
Tanganyika. A comprehensive survey of distribution, covering all traders, or at any rate a very large sample of them,
would be required. Nor is it possible to make many generalisations about the average size of stocks in relation to turnover.
This varies enormously according to the individual circumstances of the trader, the exact lines he deals in, the regularity of demand and of supply, the distance from the sources of
supply, the problems of financing stocks and so on. Figures
of stock-turn must be related to the particular circumstances
of the trader concerned.

Seasonal variations

The most striking feature of the stock position of traders
in Tanganyika is the very great variation in the amount of
stocks which many traders have to hold during the season and
during the rest of the year. The season in most areas is
roughly from June to December, though there are considerable
local variations. In particular the peak months, perhaps two
or three out of the six, vary in different areas, in accordance
with the harvesting of the locally grown crops. The slackest
period in almost all areas is from January to March.

Some areas and some types of trade are obviously more
affected than others by seasonal factors. Tanga Region is

certainly the least affected by seasonal influences followed by
the Eastern Region. These two regions are more heavily dependent on the plantation crop of sisal, which has no particular harvesting period. In Tanga Region the main seasonal
variation is a reduction in sales to the African market of perhaps 20 to 25 per cent during the rains in April and May,
otherwise trade is almost steady for the rest of the year.
Trade in the Eastern Region fluctuates more than this, since
the economy of the area is not so heavily committed to sisal;
other crops such as maize, rice, cotton, cashew nuts, sunflower, castor seeds and onions are also grown.

The Southern Region is much the most heavily affected by
seasonal variations. This is not so much because sales are
very much higher in the season than in other areas, but because sales in the out-of-season period are practically nil.
Over large areas trade comes to an almost total standstill,
mainly because of the very great difficulties involved in transporting goods during the rains. The result is that it is quite
normal for the October and November sales of a small shop
selling piecegoods in a trading centre to be ten times those of
January and February.

There does not seem to be a great deal to choose between
the other regions in the extent to which they are affected by
the seasons, though clearly certain areas will be more
affected than others. In general, retail sales to the consumers in the towns are least affected, since they are mostly
dependent on salaries paid all the year round. Fluctuations
here follow a monthly cycle, since almost all wages are paid
by the month, at the end of the month, though some are paid
in the middle of the month. On the other hand the trade of
urban wholesalers whose principal activity is supplying retailers in the rural areas is subject to seasonal variation.

Certain lines are very much more heavily affected by the
seasons than others. Among the major lines, sales of piecegoods fluctuate most heavily. In many areas sales of piecegoods in the peak months are three or four times what they
are during the rest of the year, and during the slack months
of January, February and March sales can drop to almost
nothing. As a very broad generalisation, it can be said that
sales of piecegoods roughly double in most rural areas for a
period of three to four months in the year, though in most
parts of the Southern Region the variation is much greater
than this. Clearly these variations in sales must be reflected
in similar variations in the volume of stocks held, though it is
not normally necessary to increase stocks in the same propor-

tion, as most traders are able to achieve a more rapid turn -
over, which keeps the level of stocks down. Similarly, in the
Southern Region when sales come to a standstill during the
rains, it is not possible to reduce stocks to the same extent.
Peak stock levels are often three times higher than those of
the slack season. In other areas a doubling of stocks of piecegoods at the beginning of the season is very common.

Many small traders in the remoter areas do not bother to
stock any piecegoods at all for six months of the year, except
unsold items from the previous season. A shop which looks
bare in January, apparently selling only a few foodstuffs, cigarettes and medicaments, is transformed in June or July,
with an array of khangas draped from various vantage points,
and a fair selection of materials on shelves which were empty
six months before. Clearly at this level stocks have very
much more than doubled.

Of the goods sold to the African consumers, foodstuffs are
on the whole the least affected by seasonal variations. But
there are considerable differences in different areas. In the
Eastern Region sales of locally grown foodstuffs drop by perhaps 40 per cent in the season, though sales of imported provisions rise. The drop in sales of locally grown foodstuffs
would be more if there were not a rise in sales of sugar,
mainly used for brewing local beer.

In parts of the Lake Region on the other hand sales of foodstuffs rise in the season, in some areas by as much as 50 per
cent. Much of this is accounted for by sugar. But the rise
is also the result of many farmers going over to the growing
of cash crops, and relying on purchases of foodstuffs from
outside. In other areas the sales of foodstuffs are fairly
steady all the year round, though if there is a poor harvest,
local supplies tend to run short in the period from December
to April, and sales increase during these months.

In the very large Tabora District sales of foodstuffs rise by
about 50 per cent in the out-of-season period. The fluctuation
would be even more if sales of sugar did not take place mainly
during the season. Thus in the foodstuffs trade, sales are
almost entirely of sugar and imported provisions during the
season, while out-of-season sales are mainly of the staple
Tanganyika-grown foodstuffs.

In the Moshi-Arusha area sales of provisions, mainly the
imported items, rise by about 15 to 20 per cent during July to
December. In the Central Region peak sales take place from
June to August or September, when total business roughly
doubles. Sales are also higher than average in the succeeding

months, September to December. As all the main wholesalers
in Dodoma, the commercial centre of the region, deal in both
piecegoods and provisions, it is difficult to discover the increase in sales of each of the various lines. Sales of piece -
goods undoubtedly increase the most. Sales of provisions,
mainly sugar and the imported lines, increase perhaps by 50
to 60 per cent.

In the Southern Region there is the usual increase during
the season in sales of provisions imported from outside the
region, including sugar, while sales of local foodstuffs are
negligible except in the towns. In the months of December to
February or March, sales of imported lines drop, but sales
of local foodstuffs increase considerably in the up-country
areas. This is practically the only trade which continues
through these months in many areas in the Southern Region.

In many parts of Tanganyika where the local produce is
marketed by the co-operatives there are two distinct peak
periods, one spread over several weeks or months, when the
first payments for the crops are made as they are brought in;
the second is usually comparatively short and sharp at the end
of the produce season, when the final payment is made by each
co-operative.

A few comparatively small areas have their own separate
seasons, which may run counter to those of the surrounding
districts. Examples of this are the areas in Iringa and Njombe
Districts where bamboo wine is prepared. Numerous fairly
small and scattered areas rely on this almost entirely for
their cash income. The season is roughly from January to
June or July, and thus is out of step with other crops. Similarly in Chunya District, the best fishing season in Lake Rukwa is from December to April, and trade is considerably
more brisk in that period.

In addition to the overall seasonal fluctuations in the sales
of piecegoods and provisions lines, certain special lines also
show very marked fluctuations. Sales of beer, soft drinks
and cigarettes increase considerably during the season. As
an example, in the Musoma District three times as much beer
and soft drinks are sold in-season as out-of-season. In most
rural areas, sales of cigarettes at least double in the produce
season, and in many places increase by four or five times.

Outside the towns and the areas where there are plantations,
sales of consumer durables, such as bicycles and radios, are
confined almost entirely to the produce season. Sales of
motor vehicles are also affected by the seasons, particularly
those of lorries and buses, which show a sharp rise in July

and August. Sales of agricultural machinery are also well
up in the months of July to October.

Sales of building materials are markedly seasonal, the
lines most affected being corrugated iron sheets and paint.
For Tanganyika as a whole the main season is May to October.
Again, outside the towns, sales of building materials to private consumers are entirely confined to the produce season.
In the five or six months of the season, sales of building
materials in most areas are about three times as great as
during the rest of the year.

Some items have their own peculiar seasonal variations.
In most areas sales of khaki drill used for school uniforms,
rise considerably at the beginning of the school year in
January and to a lesser extent in May after the long school
holidays. Sales of vermicelli are confined to the month of
Ramadam, mainly in the coastal areas.

These seasonal variations in sales clearly have a considerable effect on the quantity of stocks held by different types
of traders. Stocks of piecegoods are the most affected among
the bulk lines, though naturally stocks of produce rise even
more dramatically in the season. This is not because of increased demand, except to a very small extent, but because
the stocks of produce dealers, who are buying from the
growers, increase steeply.

Some typical examples of increases in stocks during the
season for different types of traders in different areas are
given below. The stocks of most of the large importer/whole-
salers of piecegoods in Dar es Salaam are built up to about
twice their normal level in the period May to August. They
are usually allowed to drop to an abnormally low level in
December, so that the increase between December and, say,
June is sometimes as much as threefold.

In the main centres up-country the stocks of mixed wholesalers, dealing mainly in piecegoods but also in provisions
and perhaps some building materials etc., are normally
double or a little more in the season than they are in the lowest month, usually January. On the other hand the stocks of
wholesaler/retailers catering mainly for the urban market
seldom increase by more than about 25 per cent. These traders include those who sell groceries and clothing for the
European and Asian market.

If a wholesaler in an up-country centre is mainly dealing
in foodstuffs and provisions, it is unlikely that his stocks will
increase by more than 50 per cent, usually by about 25 to 30
per cent. If demand increases in these lines it is usually

possible to speed up turnover considerably and thus keep
stock increases down.

Stock-turn of importers and wholesalers

The large importing houses specialising mainly in capital
goods or consumer durables turn over their stock about twice
a year, while a large importing house carrying a wide range
of agency lines, mostly consumer goods, such as piecegoods,
provisions, building materials and phamaceuticals etc., has
a stock-turn of eight times a year. A firm specialising in
imported foods has a stock-turn of five times a year. How -
ever, there is a big difference in the stock-turn of different
lines. Frozen foods imported from abroad have a very low
rate of stock-turn, while tinned foods from Kenya, which can
be delivered without delay, have a very rapid rate of stock-turn.

The stock-turn of a general importing house carrying a
varied selection of goods, including piecegoods, provisions,
paints, cement and office equipment, is about four times a
year. But here again there is a tremendous variation between
different lines, for instance, between cement from Kenya and
office equipment from abroad.

A firm in Dar es Salaam specialising entirely in the importing of building materials and builders' supplies has a stock -
turn of five times a year. Clearly cement will move very
much more rapidly than some of the little used builders' supplies.

The importers of the bulk lines of piecegoods have a stock-
turn of about ten times a year, some even more. On the other
hand the one or two fairly large firms which specialise in importing fancy goods have a stock-turn of only four times a
year. Firms which import partly bulk lines and partly fancy
lines have a stock-turn of six or eight times a year. A firm
specialising in sundries lines, such as household linen, cutlery, clocks, shoes, etc., may turn over its stock only three
times a year, while a small firm importing cheap ready-
made clothing turns over its stock about four times a year.

An importer/wholesaler in Dar es Salaam specialising in
provisions and spices has a stock-turn of fourteen times a
year, while a big importer/wholesaler of foodstuffs, who is
also a distributor for one of the local millers has a stock -
turn of twenty times a year.

Outside Dar es Salaam, in the main centres, we find also
a great divergence in the rate of stock-turn. Let us look first
at those wholesalers who are dealing mainly in piecegoods,
though seldom to the exclusion of other lines.

In Tanga two piecegoods wholesalers, dealing in the rather

more fancy lines, (sales of americani, black material etc., are probably less in Tanga Region than in any other) both turned over their stocks about ten times a year. A dealer in more sundry lines has a stock-turn of eight times a year.

In Mwanza a wholesaler dealing mainly in bulk lines has a stock-turn of sixteen times, while a wholesaler specialising in the more expensive lines of piecegoods and the cheaper clothing has a stock-turn of four times only. A retailer selling clothing to the European market may turn over his stock only one and a half times a year.

A big wholesaler doing half his business in fast-moving piecegoods and the rest mainly in foodstuffs and provisions, but also building materials, has a stock-turn of fifteen times a year. In Malampaka in Maswa district, a small wholesaler doing a similar type of business has a stock-turn of nine times a year. In Shinyanga a wholesaler who adds petrol to these lines has a stock-turn of almost twenty times a year.

In Moshi a large wholesaler, doing about two thirds of his business in piecegoods and the rest in provisions, has a stock-turn of twelve times, while in Arusha the figure for a similar wholesaler is fifteen times. Figures of this order, twelve to fifteen times, are recorded for similar wholesalers in places as widely separated as Dodoma, Lindi and Mbeya. In Tunduru in the Southern Region the figure dropped to eleven times for a wholesaler of this type, even though he adds petrol to the other lines, which must raise his stock-turn to some extent.

The average small sub-wholesaler/retailer in a trading centre, selling mostly piecegoods, has a stock-turn of about five or six times a year. However, if he is doing a large part of his business as a sub-wholesaler this figure rises to about ten times a year. A small retailer, specialising in piece-goods in a main centre, probably employing some tailors, usually has a lower stock-turn, of about three times a year. However, the very small Arab and Asian piecegoods retailers in the main centres, obtaining most of their supplies from a local wholesaler and working on a very low margin with a very small stock, may have a stock-turn as high as eight or nine times a year. These traders are really relying on the stock of the wholesaler, and are in effect the retail branches of his business, since they probably obtain most of their supplies from him on a system of continuous credit.

Turning to foodstuffs and provisions wholesalers, we find a big wholesaler in Tanga, with a large business in sugar, turning over his stock twenty times a year, while a whole -

saler in imported sundry provisions lines, carrying a wide
range of goods, has a stock-turn of eight times a year.   In
Mwanza the stock-turn of a wholesaler whose main line   is
sugar is as high as twenty three times a year.   In Shinyanga
a general foodstuffs and provisions wholesaler, able to draw
also on stocks from a head office in Mwanza, has a stock-turn
of fifteen times, while in Singida an independent wholesaler
of this type has a stock-turn of eleven times.   In Moshi the
equivalent figure is thirteen times.

However, for individual businesses there are great variations.   In Musoma a wholesaler doing two-thirds of his business in provisions, and with a beer agency which accounts
for half of his wholesale turnover, turns over his stock only
eight times a year, but a third of this total turnover is in
builders' supplies, which are slow-moving and reduce his
average rate of stock-turn.   A wholesaler in Mbulu in the
Northern Region, selling mainly provisions, much of them
on contract, but also building materials and petrol, turns
over his stock fifteen times a year.   From these examples
it will be seen that the combinations of goods which a wholesaler of this type can sell are numerous and have a profound
effect on his rate of stock-turn.

Another very important consideration is the length of time
that supplies take to be delivered in different areas.   For
instance, in Mwanza a large wholesaler dealing in various
lines has almost a third of his total stocks tied up in transit.
On the other hand, at Moshi only a very small proportion of
stocks is in the pipeline, as delivery from Mombasa is very
quick.   A building materials merchant in Moshi has a stock-
turn of nine times a year, because of his ability to order
quickly from Mombasa, while in Dodoma this figure was reduced to only six times a year for a merchant in a similar
business.   In the more distant areas this problem is a very
serious one.   Supplies normally take a month at least to
reach Songea, for instance, and this means that a high proportion of stocks is always in transit.   This reduces the
rate of stock-turn very considerably, and is an important
factor in increasing the margins charged in such remote
areas.

Stock-turn of retailers

Retailers also show a wide variation in the rate of stock-
turn.   A general provisions retailer selling to the African
market in Dar es Salaam turns over his stock about twenty
times a year, while another similar retailer about five
miles from the centre of town, turns his over about fifteen

times a year. A similar small general provisions store, but
also stocking some piecegoods, at a flourishing small market
centre such as Mamba, near Marangu in Moshi District, has
a stock-turn of about ten times a year. This seems to be
about an average figure for shops of this type away from the
towns and trading centres.

The rate of stock-turn of the really small retailers depends
very much on the demand in their locality and the availability
of transport. The amount of stock held by these small re -
tailers is to some extent fixed by the minimum quantities of the
standard goods which they can buy at wholesale prices, i.e.,
a sack, a tin, a carton of cigarettes or aspirin or a bag of
sweets. As fast as these are consumed, the retailer has to
buy another sack, tin or carton.

This system can of course present serious problems, as
the different items are consumed at different rates. If the
journey to the wholesaler or sub-wholesaler is a long one, it
can only be made perhaps once a month, but a sack of one of
the fast-selling items may be consumed long before then.
However, the cost of a journey to buy one sack is likely to be
prohibitive, so that many small retailers frequently find themselves out of stock of some of their best-selling lines for quite
long periods at a time.

There are two measures which wholesalers could take to
solve this problem. One would be for more of them to send
round lorries selling from shop to shop. However, we have
already seen that there are serious problems connected with
this, though perhaps with good organisation these are not as
insuperable as is sometimes made out. The other is for more
wholesalers and sub-wholesalers to sell half sacks of the
foodstuffs items. It is usually sugar, rice and maize meal,
which have to be bought by the sack, that cause the problem
for the small retailer. It would be a great help if these items
were more often available in half sacks. It is interesting in
this connection to note that the one or two wholesalers inter -
viewed in the course of this survey who had recently started
this practice reported exceptionally good business.

THE FINANCING OF WHOLESALE AND RETAIL TRADE

A feature of the trade in Tanganyika, as in East Africa as
a whole, is its extreme dependence at almost all stages on
credit. A very large part of all traders' supplies are obtained
on credit, and the amount of working capital employed by most

traders is extremely small. The volume of credit reached a
peak in 1959, since when the amount has been steadily cut
down, and an increasing part of trade has gone over to a cash
basis. Nevertheless, in 1961 the amount of credit given by
suppliers of all sorts was still very large.

There are in effect six sources of finance for the trade in
Tanganyika. Credit for varying periods can be obtained by
importers from overseas suppliers. Imports can be financed
through London confirming houses. Many of the importing
houses in Tanganyika are financed in one way or another by
their head offices abroad. Some credit for locally produced
goods can be obtained from the manufacturers. Finance can
be obtained from the local banks in the form of an overdraft
or by discounting bills. Finally the traders themselves provide some of their own working capital inside the trading
system.

It is unfortunately quite impossible to give any estimates
of the amount of finance obtained from these various sources,
except to say that in March, 1962, loans by the commercial
banks under the heading Trade and Transport came to $9.3
million. No more detailed break-down of this figure is available. A large part was accounted for by loans to the motor
trade. A further large part was taken up by loans and advances to produce brokers and exporters. It is, therefore,
quite impossible to say with any accuracy what proportion
was in respect of loans and advances to wholesalers and retailers, but perhaps it might have been between $3.4 million
and $4.2 million. This does not cover more than a small part
of the trade. Finance from the local banks plays a much bigger role proportionately in produce marketing than in distributive trading. Credit from overseas suppliers, from confirming houses and from the importing firms with overseas
head office undoubtedly supplies most of the finance to the
trade.

Much of the finance comes from abroad, and the successive
wholesalers, sub-wholesalers and retailers in Tanganyika are
heavily dependent on credit from their respective suppliers.
Thus finance percolates down from the top to the bottom of
the system, becoming increasingly costly in the process.
Very little external finance is injected into the system from
outside sources at the lower levels. The banks, the most important source of credit, give very much the largest part of it,
though not by any means all, to the importers and bigger wholesalers near the top of the system. The multitude of small
traders in the sub-wholesale and retail classes are heavily

dependent on their various suppliers for finance.

This is of course the usual pattern in the less developed countries, but is in sharp contrast to the situation in England, for instance. There wholesalers and retailers, right down to the bottom of the distributive chain, obtain a large part of their finance from sources other than their suppliers. Their own sources are usually quite large. Many concerns, including retailers, are public companies able to raise finance on the open market, and almost all of them are able to obtain finance in one form or another from the banks.

In Tanganyika most traders have very limited resources indeed. Scarcely any, other than a few of the importers, are public companies, and few are able to consider obtaining finance from the banks. It is generally felt that the banks could do more than they do at present to finance small traders. They are, however, faced with very great difficulties in this field: for instance, there are only 50 full-time branch banks in Tanganyika, and there is undoubtedly not enough banking business for many more than this. In 1961 there were 48,535 licensed wholesalers and retailers in Tanganyika. This means that there was one branch bank to every 970 traders, while in the United Kingdom there is one branch bank to every 50 wholesalers and retailers. Most traders in Tanganyika are too small to consider obtaining credit from the banks. Very few of them even have bank accounts, though undoubtedly more could be encouraged to do so.

As might be expected, less credit is given by importers and wholesalers on the fast-moving lines than on the slow-moving ones. Most of the fast-moving bulk lines are either sold for cash or on short-term credit, seldom more than 30 days. This tendency has increased in the last few years, and local manufacturers in particular have been steadily cutting down the credit they give on such items as soap, maize meal and beer. This means that the traders in their turn have cut down the credit given on these lines, and have gone over to cash terms as far as possible.

In the foodstuffs and provisions trade, perhaps 50 per cent of the business is now on cash at the wholesale level, where three years ago cash sales were probably only 20 per cent of the total or less. Now sugar and soap are entirely on a cash basis, as well as a great deal of the trade in such lines as rice, tinned milk, etc. Much of the rest is on 30 days only.

However, practically all the trade in the slower moving lines is still on credit, but whereas terms of 120 days used to be quite common, now they seldom exceed 90 days, except

in the building trade, and much of the business is done on 60
days or less. Most traders have reduced their total credit
outstanding. This has been done partly by reducing the length
of credit given, but probably more by cutting down each customer's credit limit. In many cases these limits have been
halved.

But in spite of all this, probably between 85 and 90 per cent
of all the piecegoods sold by the big wholesalers are on credit,
usually 90 days. Up-country the smaller wholesalers probably
do about 60 per cent of their business on credit, but this varies
very much according to individual circumstances.

The amount of credit obtained by retailers from wholesalers
varies enormously. Retailers supplying the European market
for foodstuffs or clothing obtain most of their supplies on credit. The retailers specialising in piecegoods for the Asian and
African market also obtain most of their supplies on credit.
The general store in a trading centre doing both sub-wholesaling and retailing probably on average obtains 50 per cent
of its supplies on credit, but this is a very broad generalisation, and there are great variations. A general store doing a
purely retail business is normally able to obtain between 20
and 30 per cent of its supplies on credit. The very small
African retailers with sales of less than $1,400 a year are
seldom able to obtain any supplies on credit.

It is frequently said that the wholesalers and sub-wholesalers, who are almost entirely Asian or Arab, discriminate
against African retailers in the matter of giving credit. This
feeling is very widespread among African traders themselves.
It is undoubtedly true that very few of the thousands of very
small African traders receive any credit from their suppliers.
However, it is equally certain that this is not a question of
discrimination against African retailers as such. The risks
involved in giving credit to such very small and almost always
inexperienced traders are too great for any supplier, of whatever race, to undertake. The goods which these small retailers want to obtain on credit are almost always the fast-
moving lines, on which wholesale margins are very slender.
If a wholesaler supplies a $21 bag of rice on credit he runs a
grave risk of losing the whole sum. He makes little profit to
compensate for this risk, and he is unlikely to increase his
total sales greatly. On the other hand if the retailer fails to
meet his obligations, the wholesaler is likely to lose his custom entirely, since the retailer will in future go to other
wholesalers.

Many of the larger African retailers obtain part of their

supplies on credit, mainly piecegoods, and often, as we have seen, at considerable extra cost. The African retailers in the more remote areas on the other hand, even if they are quite large, often find it difficult to get credit. These African retailers feel that more Asian retailers get credit, that they get more of their supplies on credit and that they get cheaper credit.

There is a considerable tangle of misunderstandings in all this, as well as a fair element of truth. No wholesaler is prepared to give credit to a retailer of whatever race, European, Asian, or African, if he does not know him and consider him credit-worthy. The Asian retailers obtain credit because they are old-established customers. An African retailer who has done business on a cash basis for some time and proved himself reliable will almost certainly obtain credit in exactly the same way as an Asian retailer.

In general the reason why African retailers get less credit is because they are genuinely less credit-worthy. They constitute a greater risk to the wholesaler giving credit. Their shops are smaller and they usually have much less business experience. If they default the Asian wholesaler has very little hope of receiving eventual payment. It must be admitted, however, that many Asian wholesalers are in fact more ready to assume risks in the case of a fellow Asian. This is an unfortunate fact, but it is only natural in the circumstances, since the wholesaler is likely to know more about the financial and family background of the fellow Asian retailer, and therefore can more easily judge his credit-worthiness. Perhaps more important, if the Asian retailer defaults, the wholesaler can bring various social pressures to bear on him, short of legal action, which he cannot bring to bear on an African trader. It is also true that many small Asian retailers, mainly in the towns, receive credit from wholesalers only because they are prepared to pay crippling rates for it. An African retailer would probably not be prepared to accept these.

Three years ago, when credit was much more freely available than it is now, many Asian traders, particularly in the Lake Region, began to give credit to a much larger number of African retailers. However, with the credit squeeze which has been in force for the last two years or more, these facilities have almost all been withdrawn, and this has undoubtedly caused resentment among many African retailers. There was a large element of competitive credit-giving in this wave of credit to African retailers in 1958 and 1959. Much of it was very risky, and many bad debts were incurred. A more careful expansion of credit to African retailers seems desirable.

Many Asian wholesalers might benefit from visiting the shops of their African retailer customers, instead of sitting more or less permanently in their own stores, and merely seeing the African trader when he comes in to buy. More about the credit-worthiness of the retailer could be discovered from one visit to his shop than from a hundred transactions carried out on the wholesaler's own premises.

CHAPTER **5** AN ASSESSMENT
OF THE
DISTRIBUTION SYSTEM

A LOW-COST DISTRIBUTION SYSTEM

We have already seen in the section dealing with margins
that the average costs of distribution in Tanganyika are low.
In the same way that some manufacturers are low-cost producers, so, taken as a whole, the distribution system in
Tanganyika is a low-cost distribution system. This is taking
the overall picture: the costs of distributing certain goods
are very high, but those of distributing bulk commodities are
extremely low, and this brings the average down.

How are low costs of distribution achieved in the face of
the great distances that have to be covered, the poor communications, the low purchasing power and sparse population,
and the very wide seasonal variations in supply and demand?
The most important reasons seem to be: wage levels are low
in Tanganyika, and distribution is a labour-intensive industry;
most traders manage to keep their overheads down to the very
minimum, and finally the level of income expected is not high
by West European or American standards.

Traditional methods of distribution require a great deal of
labour, both for handling the goods and for serving in the
shops, hence the trend towards self-service stores in countries where labour costs are high. Self-service stores would
not be economic in Tanganyika, since the costs involved in
installing the necessary display equipment etc., and the costs
of repacking all the goods normally sold loose would far exceed any possible savings in the wages of sales staff. Not
only is the level of wages paid in Tanganyika low, but the
earnings to be obtained from occupations other than shop-
keeping are in general low; thus most shopkeepers are prepared to carry on a small retail business in return for a very
low level of income indeed.

The overhead costs of almost all wholesalers and retailers
in Tanganyika, with the general exception of the European-
owned firms, are kept to the minimum by a variety of means.
In the first place, almost all businesses are family businesses;
in comparatively few does the number of paid employees exceed

the number of working family members. These family mem -
bers are prepared to work extremely long hours, and it is this
factor which helps to keep down the overheads which would
otherwise be incurred by the extremely seasonal nature of
most of the trade. At the height of the season, when the
volume of business may treble or quadruple, it is a matter of
all family hands to the pump, and on many occasions they will
be working as much as eighteen hours a day.

Overheads are also reduced by keeping all forms of paper
work to a minimum. Most businesses keep no accounts of any
sort; when accounts are kept they are usually of the sketchiest.
Only the comparatively large firms maintain a proper account-
ing system, and practically none keep any form of stock re -
cords. The cost of fitting out most traders' premises is not
high: some wooden shelves, a counter and a pair of scales,
if a retailer; some more extensive wooden shelves, a desk,
two chairs, a weighing machine and a store behind the shop,
if a wholesaler. Even some of the largest wholesalers in Dar
es Salaam often have little more than this, though they may
have more extensive storage facilities.

The costs of delivery are usually negligible since on the
rare occasions when this service is provided a charge is
normally made. The costs of transport of supplies are of
course usually high, but the figures for gross margins given
above have all been net of transport, so that this does not have
to be considered. Expenses of advertising, display or sales
aids of any sort are usually nil.

THE STATE OF COMPETITION

Competition in both wholesaling and retailing in Tanganyika
is generally very intense indeed, though there are of course
exceptions. It is the natural and almost universal desire of
both producers and distributors the world over to reduce the
amount of competition as much as possible. This is as true
of Tanganyika as anywhere else, but on the whole efforts to
reduce competition in Tanganyika are not outstandingly successful. Competition can normally be reduced by the various competitors coming to an agreement among themselves, by effect-
ing amalgamations or by achieving a monopoly position in some
other way.

Lasting agreements between traders to reduce the amount
of competition are seldom achieved in Tanganyika. Partly this

is because traders are drawn from a great variety of racial
and religious communities, which tend to be suspicious of
each other. But perhaps more important is the general lack
of trust between traders, even if they are of the same community. The habit of driving a hard bargain and gaining a temporary financial advantage, even if it is at the expense of possible long-term gains, is so ingrained that few traders can
bring themselves to stick for long to any agreement which
restricts their freedom to do this.

Amalgamations between traders seem to be almost unknown.
Again a lack of trust seems to be mainly responsible. The
splitting of existing partnerships, so that one or more part-
ners can set up a new business, is very much more common
than the reverse process. Monopoly positions are occasionally
achieved, as, for instance, by chemists or builder's supplies
merchants in certain areas. But monopolies are exceptional
and in most cases do not last long. Entry into most types of
business is far too open for monopoly profits to be long-
lasting. The most promising fields for the establishment of
monopolies are those trades which require large amounts of
capital. Capital is generally short in Tanganyika, and anyone
who possesses it can often obtain exceptional returns.

Produce trading needs large sums of capital, and it is in
this field that monopoly, or rather oligopoly, conditions are
often established. In most areas in Tanganyika there are not
more than five or six large produce buyers, often only one or
two, and they usually seem to be able to come to an agreement
not to cut each other's throat.

In most areas produce buying is very much less competitive
than wholesaling and retailing. As more capital is needed to
set up successfully as a produce buyer than as a retailer or
even usually as a wholesaler, so entry into the field of produce
buying is much more difficult, and existing buyers enjoy a
certain degree of protection.

In wholesaling and retailing, local monopoly or oligopoly
positions are of course established by traders in certain lines
in limited areas in different parts of Tanganyika. Because
of the difficulties of communication and the small size of the
market, traders are sometimes able to obtain excessively
high margins on certain slow-moving lines. This is bound to
happen in all distribution systems, but in Tanganyika the sections of the trade where competition is seriously reduced for
any length of time are small. Occasionally it happens that
all the piecegoods wholesalers in a medium-sized centre are
related and are able to raise prices slightly. However, they

are seldom able to raise them by very much, as retailers are
always able to go to the next centre, say 50 or 80 miles away,
and buy their supplies at the normal competitive prices.

The area where there seems to be the most widespread
reduction in competition in wholesaling and retailing is the
Southern Region. The trade in the Southern Region is very
much less competitive, and prices are on the whole higher
there than in any other large area in Tanganyika. There
seem to be two reasons for this. As has already been ex -
plained, produce trading and distributive trading are more
closely linked in the Southern Region than elsewhere.
Secondly, the region's communications with the rest of Tanganyika are worse than those of any other large area. The pro -
duce buyers have a very strong grip on the whole trade of the
region through the system of branch shops. It is very difficult
for small independent retailers to set up successfully in competition with these branches, which are backed by the much
larger resources of the produce buyers/wholesalers. As a
result, there are many fewer traders in most of the districts
of the Southern Region than in the rest of Tanganyika. In at
least two of the minor centres in the Southern Region, some
agreement to reduce competition and raise prices seems to
have been reached between the comparatively small number
of wholesalers trading in each.

However, these conditions are likely to change now that
the marketing of the main local crop, cashew nuts, has been
taken over by the co-operatives as from this year. As we
have seen, it is seldom worth the while of the produce-buyer
to maintain a system of branch shops if he is no longer able
to buy most of the local produce through them.

The coast road from Lindi to Dar es Salaam is the only
land-link between the Southern Region and the rest of Tanganyika, except for an enormously circuitous route through Songea, Njombe and Iringa. For almost six months of the year
the Lindi-Dar es Salaam road is impassable and the only
communications are by sea. Coastal steamer services are
comparatively infrequent. Schooners provide the only really
frequent service, and here one firm in the Southern Region
has managed to establish itself in a semi-monopoly position,
with a special arrangement covering three out of the four
schooners operating. This position is certainly not a full -
scale monopoly, since other traders are still able to use the
fourth, somewhat unreliable, schooner and the infrequent
steamer services. Nevertheless the arrangement acts to
restrict competition and raise prices. An all-weather road

from Lindi to Dar es Salaam would not only open up the
region and bring it into the main stream of development in
Tanganyika, it would also increase competition in the trade
of the region and help greatly to reduce the general level of
prices.

The European-based importing houses, mostly with their
local head offices in Dar es Salaam, tend to frown - as do
their principals - on cut-throat competition. They feel,
rightly no doubt in many instances, that cut-throat price
competition is not always to the benefit of the consumer -
that it frequently leads to a reduction in quality, in the
services provided, in reliability and regularity of supplies
and so on. Nevertheless there seems little doubt that the
overheads of some of these importing houses are high. It
has on occasion been found possible to cut the numbers of
rather costly expatriate staff without greatly reducing the
turnover or the standard of service provided. There is also
undoubtedly an element of restriction and even monopoly in
many of the agencies held by these firms. In many lines the
market is small; one agency can obtain a dominating position, and may be tempted to exploit this. Evidence of this
occurred recently when a big contract for four-wheel drive
vehicles in East Africa went to the only other serious rival
in the field, with the result that the agents for a well-known
make almost halved the price of their spare parts a few
days later.

In general, it can be said with complete certainty that the
distribution system in Tanganyika is one of the most competitive on price of any system in the world. Like all distribution systems, it has sectors where the competition is less
intense than in others, or where it may even be minimal,
but these sectors cover much less of the total trade than in
most countries, and the competition between traders in the
bulk, fast-moving lines is greater than almost anywhere else.

However, outside that part of the trade handled by the
importing houses with agency lines, competition among
traders takes the form of price-competition, practically to
the exclusion of all other forms of competition. There is
almost no competition in providing good service, pleasing
shopping conditions, display, reliability etc. Most traders
in Tanganyika are obsessed with the problem of price to the
exclusion of almost all other aspects of distribution. This
attitude has had an extremely important, and in some ways
disastrous, effect on the development of the distribution
system in Tanganyika.

THE EFFICIENCY OF THE DISTRIBUTION SYSTEM

If low costs are taken as a measure of efficiency then Tanganyika's distribution system might be assumed to be efficient.
However, there are other considerations besides cost to be
taken into account when judging a distribution system. Consumers may value quite highly such things as a polite and
agreeable shopkeeper, who will even perhaps explain the
merits of his various wares, a well-laid out shop and a pleasing display of goods. They may like to have a feeling of con-
fidence that what they are buying is of the quality and also in
the quantity that it is said to be, that if the article is found to
be faulty it will be replaced, and possibly they may like to
pay a standard price, which they know everyone else who
deals with this store pays, rather than be granted a "special"
price that is probably specially higher than their neighbour
paid a few moments before.

It may be argued that 95 per cent of Tanganyikan consumers want low prices; this is true, but it does not mean that
they do not also value courteous and efficient service. Such
service could be provided by the retailer with little extra
effort, but merely by a change in his methods of doing business; the additional turnover thus achieved would absorb any
increase in costs which he might incur and thus enable him
to maintain his price to the consumer unchanged.

It is steadfastly maintained by almost all Tanganyika traders that it is impossible to substitute fixed or standard
prices for the present almost universal system of bargaining
over purchases. It is alleged that customers enjoy bargaining for its own sake and that they would never accept a fixed
price as being the best price obtainable; they would transfer
their custom elsewhere. Observation, however, suggests
otherwise. In bargaining over any slightly unfamiliar article,
the customer usually appears to feel at a disadvantage vis-a-
vis the shopkeeper; he is distrustful of information supplied
by the seller and when he finally clinches the deal is left with
a growing doubt that he has not beaten the trader down to his
"last price" - that, in fact, he has been cheated. This is no
way to build up good relations between shopkeeper and customer; clearly the practice of bargaining is responsible for
much of the distrust with which the trading community is
viewed in most areas.

Bargaining certainly enables retailers on occasion to
obtain exceptionally high prices from some of their more

ignorant customers, and this swells their total profits by a small amount - but hardly enough to compensate for the huge reservoir of ill-will which is thereby built up. From the trader's standpoint the great advantage of fixed prices is that they would encourage a much quicker rate of turnover, and therefore, ultimately larger profits. At present each transaction tends to be a protracted affair, even if it involves only a few shillings. In the season, when a high proportion of total sales is made, this process of bargaining very much curtails each retailer's total turnover. If he were to operate a fixed price policy he would be able to increase his turnover considerably.

During the course of this survey a few wholesalers and retailers were seen who had in recent years changed over from a system of bargaining to a fixed price policy. These traders without exception maintained that as a result of the change they had increased their turnover and had captured a considerable number of customers from traders who had continued to do their business on the basis of bargaining.

However, a change to a policy of fixed prices is only one aspect of an overall change which seems to be required in the attitude of retailers to their customers. A new attitude is urgently needed whereby the customer is no longer considered as an opponent to be outwitted and, if possible, fleeced. A sound business, not only for the individual, but for the trading community as a whole, can only be built up on the basis of fair-dealing and trust between retailer and consumer. At present there are very few traders in Tanganyika who do not invariably choose the immediate quick profit in preference to a smaller profit, which, however, will build up goodwill and an expanding business in the future.

It was possible, no doubt, in the past to build up a business on the basis of always taking the quick profit. All traders pursued the same policy, and if the customer resented it, he was unable to find a trader who would give him better treatment. Formerly, perhaps it was not necessary to consider the customer's point of view or even bother to be polite to him. However, this is no longer the case. Times have changed. It is clear that in future, if a trader is to build up a sound business, he will have to consider the wishes of his customers, he will have to realise that he is providing a service for them, not conducting a never-ending battle of wits against them.

The efficiency of the wholesalers

These criticisms are directed against the retailer, but they all apply with equal force to the wholesaler and sub-whole-

saler in his dealings with the small retailer. However, there
are also various other problems which apply only in the field
of wholesaling. We have already noted (see page 77) that
the piecegoods wholesalers in Dar es Salaam have been steadily losing business to their competitors in Mombasa in the
last few years. Clearly all is not well with at least this
sector of the wholesale trade. In fact the problems facing
these wholesalers, small turnover, inadequate stocks, a
reluctance to go out and sell, etc., are part of a much larger
group of problems facing wholesalers in Tanganyika generally
at present.

Wholesalers, like retailers, are obsessed with the question
of price. They have as a result produced what is, taken as a
whole, a remarkably low-cost distribution system. However,
it cannot be said to be an efficient system. Many of the essential functions of wholesaling are not carried out at all, or only
quite inadequately, by the great majority of wholesalers in
Tanganyika.

Many wholesalers hold inadequate stocks, thus often
causing a hold-up in supplies, shortages and unnecessary
fluctuations in price. They rely on their suppliers having the
stocks, or if a large order comes in, on being able to shop
around other wholesalers, thus also raising the price unneces-
sarily.

Many are chronically addicted to over-trading. They rely
excessively on credit, and when their expectations of business
are not fulfilled, they have to unload their stocks at cut prices,
thus causing further price fluctuations. We have seen that the
trade in Tanganyika is in any case subject to wide fluctuations in
price, because of variations in the prices of overseas supplies
and because of local seasonal variations. The wholesalers do
little, if anything, to help iron out these fluctuations. More
often they are instrumental in increasing them. If there were
more wholesalers holding adequate stocks and fewer who in-
dulged in over-trading, price fluctuations would almost certainly be less than they are today.

The number of wholesalers who do an active job of selling
the lines they deal in is very small indeed. Active selling is
confined almost entirely to sending round travellers - and
only a very small proportion of all the wholesalers even in
Dar es Salaam do this - a little press advertising and, up-
country, sending round lorries to the small retailers - and
this very few wholesalers do. Otherwise, they rely on per-
sonal contacts, the system of brokers and the arrival, in the
course of time, of the retailer in their store.

Roneoed price lists may be sent out, but never illustrated catalogues. Even fewer wholesalers than retailers bother to display their range of goods attractively or to push new lines. Active promotion and publicity are almost unheard of.

Modern methods of wholesaling are almost totally unknown in Tanganyika. Few traders have ever seen modern methods of running a wholesale business in operation. The traditional methods of running a bazaar business are still the only ones understood by most wholesalers. It is noticeable, however, that standards of wholesaling in the Northern Region are appreciably higher than elsewhere. This is presumably the influence of the more up-to-date business methods which can be seen in Nairobi, particularly, but also in Mombasa.

The actual day-to-day running of the vast mass of wholesale businesses in Tanganyika is at an astonishingly low level of efficiency. Minimal accounts are normally kept, so that few wholesalers have more than a very general idea of how their businesses are really doing. The relative profitability or even volume of turnover of different lines, for instance, is almost always a matter of pure guesswork. Stock records are practically never kept. The stock position of often hundreds of items is kept in the wholesaler's head. This might not be so bad if the stocks were neatly arranged on shelves or in the godown, so that the position could be checked visually without too much difficulty. However, this is practically never the case. Goods are usually stacked higgledy-piggledy all over the shop. Perhaps the trader himself knows pretty well where everything is, and which is fresh and which is old stock; however, the general confusion does not help his potential customers to see what goods are available.

The introduction of new methods of doing business and the development of new markets are almost always extremely slow. For instance, one wholesaler in the Northern Region has recently started to import high-quality cottonseed oil and also tinned milk, and has specially printed labels with his own brand name on them. This experiment has apparently been extremely successful, but few wholesalers have yet developed the idea of selling their own branded lines. Such an idea runs counter to the accepted principle that price is all-important, and that giving some guarantee of quality is of no account. Another example of a new technique which has been slow to catch on is the very successful introduction by small wholesalers in some areas of selling half bags of foodstuffs. They do an excellent business, but the idea seems slow to spread.

There seems to be an expanding market for cheap ready-made clothing in certain styles for African customers who are beginning to earn slightly higher monthly salaries. A few traders are specially catering for this market and are doing a good business, but in most areas no effort is being made to push these lines.

The number of wholesalers who conduct a modern and efficient type of wholesaling business in Tanganyika is very small indeed. There are one or two outstanding examples. They have well laid-out premises, goods systematically stored and properly displayed and a wide range of stock. They have adopted a policy of fixed prices and of honest dealing. They admit that on occasions those wholesalers who have not adopted a fixed price policy may be able to undercut them, though on other occasions the situation may be reversed. In any case the up-to-date wholesaler has an enormous number of regular customers who deal with him exclusively. These customers prefer the good service, wide range of stock, regularity of supply, reliability of quality and steadiness of prices to the possibility of occasionally obtaining a bargain from a wholesaler who can offer none of these advantages. The up-to-date wholesaler has in each case a major and expanding share of the market in his district. The lesson is there for all to see.

Besides a change in the attitude of the trader to his customers, there is clearly room for an immense improvement in the standards and technique of wholesaling in Tanganyika. There is no reason why the country should not have both a low-cost and an efficient, progressive and expanding distribution system. This would be an extremely important stimulus to the development of the economy.

THE ECONOMIC EFFECTS OF THE SHORTCOMINGS
OF THE PRESENT DISTRIBUTION SYSTEM

It was commonly believed some years ago that the distribution network in East Africa supplied an inadequate range of consumer goods, and thus failed to provide an incentive to small farmers and workers generally to increase their cash incomes. An investigation was carried out in 1952-53 by Dr F. Chalmers Wright which fairly conclusively showed that this was not the case, and this criticism is seldom heard now. However, there seem to be several other ways in which the shortcomings of the present distribution system have adversely affected the development of the economy.

With a wide range of goods usually available even in the minor trading centres, the fault seems to lie more in the way in which they are sold. If more active salesmanship were common in Tanganyika, it seems very likely that a lot more business could be done, a stimulus would be provided to the economy, the flow of money, particularly in the rural areas, could be speeded up considerably and more incentive given to raising cash earnings. This is not only a question of more active salesmanship, more efficient methods and better display at all levels of distribution. There is a further aspect, and here again we come back to the attitude of the traders.

If, instead of treating customers as opponents, more traders took the trouble to explain honestly the differences in quality and price of their various wares and actively encouraged the potential customer to buy the goods which he could afford, there is no doubt that a great deal more business would be done. At present it is a very general policy among traders deliberately to keep their customers in the dark about differences in quality and price, particularly of piece-goods. In this way they hope to preserve an ignorance of which they will be able to take advantage. No doubt, on occasions they are rewarded with a handsome 100 per cent profit on a 70 cents length of spun cotton dress material. There is no doubt also that this policy does not exactly encourage customers to come and buy, and that it greatly reduces the traders' total volume of business. It also reduces his total income. It is practices of this sort which act as the strongest disincentive to potential customers, and, therefore, indirectly to their desire to earn bigger cash incomes.

The concentration by traders on price competition has the expected effect of leading, in far too many instances, to concealed reductions in quality and quantity. Wholesalers and retailers are always trying to supply at the cheapest possible prices. To do this they frequently resort to the passing off of lower quality goods and selling in sub-standard quantities. African consumers are undoubtedly very price-conscious, but they are quality-conscious as well. If they have the knowledge needed to judge the quality of an article, they are very interested in getting the best value for their money. The popularity of well-known branded goods, for which the brand name provides some guarantee of quality, testifies to this strong preference for good quality. Unfortunately, the trader's excessive price-consciousness often means that the

better quality lines are not stocked, and the quality-conscious-
ness of African consumers can often in this way be frustrated.

THE PROBLEM OF SHORT WEIGHTS

The practice of selling sacks of foodstuffs or tins of edible
oils which are under-weight is widespread through Tanganyika.
It is, of course, impossible to say how widespread. For one
thing, very few of the retailers have the sacks that they buy
weighed. There are various reasons for this. One is that
most retailers do not think in terms of buying a certain specific weight. They buy by the sack or by the tin. They judge
the amount by the appearance. Retailers seldom realise how
much several pounds or kilos short-weight in a sack can
affect their own margins. They tend to be much more price-
conscious than weight-conscious, and this is another characteristic which wholesalers frequently take advantage of.

As there are no laws in East Africa to enforce standard
weights for the sale of any foodstuffs, other than bread,
wholesalers are perfectly at liberty to sell by the sack or by
the tin without specifying any weights. They are thus able to
offer sacks at cheap prices, because they contain smaller
quantities. This is perfectly well-known, but small retailers
are nevertheless attracted by what appears to be a bargain.

A further element of confusion is added by the use of both
the imperial and metric systems side by side, i.e. pounds
and kilos, as well as various local measures, such as the
frasila (36 pounds, though by no means standard throughout
the country) pishi and kibaba, 4 litres and 1 litre respectively. These last are measures of capacity not weight. All
this would be enough to confuse the most sophisticated small
retailer. In fact in many cases the use of these numerous
different measures seems deliberately designed to confuse.

A great many of the scales used in Tanganyika are inaccu-
rate. The Weights and Measures Inspectorate of the Ministry
of Commerce and Industry is short of staff. Much of their
time is taken up with checking the weighing apparatus belong-
ing to the producers' co-operative societies. The weighing
apparatus of traders in many areas has not been checked within the last five years. Spot checks on apparatus on traders'
premises are seldom made, because of the lack of staff.

However, all this would be a more serious problem than it
is now if it were the normal practice for retailers to have

their purchases from wholesalers weighed. But it is not the
normal practice. At present it is more important for the retailer to have a sharp eye for an under-weight sack, than for
a wholesaler to have an accurate weighing machine. Most
wholesalers carefully keep their weighing machines out of
sight in the back of the store, unless they happen to be buying
produce as well as wholesaling foodstuffs. Most retailers do
not bother to go to the trouble of insisting that the weighing
machine be produced. Even if a request for a sack to be
weighed is made, it is normally refused by the wholesaler,
and the retailer has to go elsewhere until he finds a wholesaler with sacks which appear to be the correct weight. In
many areas there is tacit agreement among wholesalers that
all requests for foodstuffs to be weighed should be refused.

Many retailers reported from all parts of the country that
when sacks are weighed they are frequently found to be two
or three kilos short and sometimes more. The normal practice then is for the wholesaler to make the necessary adjust-
ment to the price.

These widespread abuses are to a large extent brought
about by the intense competition which prevails in the wholesaling of foodstuffs. It must be quite laborious spending one's
evenings in the godown inserting a length of bamboo into every
sack and draining off a few kilos from each. No doubt if a
better margin could be obtained without resorting to this practice, many wholesalers, though not all, would abandon it. In
any case the present state of the law, the regulations, and
their enforcement constitute an open invitation to indulge in
these practices and to exploit the gullibility of the average
small retailer.

Certain quite simple measures could be introduced which
would greatly reduce this problem of short weights. Legisla-
tion is required to lay down and enforce standard weights for
the sacks of the various types of produce and for the tins of
cooking oils. It would be desirable that these weights should
all be in terms of one system, preferably, the imperial system, as this is at present the most commonly used. In the
second place, it could be made compulsory for every wholesaler selling goods by weight to have his weighing apparatus
easily accessible in the front of his shop, and it might be made
an offence for him to refuse to allow the goods to be weighed.
Finally, at least one weights and measures inspector should
carry out random spot checks of weighing apparatus in every
district at least once a year. It would not be necessary to
examine more than a small selection at random in each area.

If the existing provision in the Traders Licensing Ordinance
that disqualifies anyone convicted of an offence under the
Weights and Measures Ordinance from obtaining a licence
were rigorously enforced, it would be a powerful deterrent to
traders indulging in false weights.

If the present widespread malpractices in relation to
weights were stamped out, or at any rate greatly reduced, by
the measures suggested above, it seems likely that in many
cases the prices of foodstuffs would have to rise by a dollar
or   so a bag, if many wholesalers were not to be driven completely out of business. A great deal of competition has undoubtedly taken the form of reducing weights. The elimination
of this would lead to an apparent rise in prices, but it must be
emphasised that this rise would be only apparent and not real.

THE POSITION OF AFRICAN TRADERS

Over two-thirds of all the traders licensed in Tanganyika
in 1961 were Africans, yet these traders almost certainly did
less than one-third of the total business. They are almost all
small traders, and only a handful does any wholesale business.
The question arises, why have Africans not made more progress in trade?

Africans started to enter trade only comparatively recently.
There were very few African traders in Tanganyika in the
1930s. The big increase in numbers has come in the last
twenty years. Originally few Africans were able to collect
together the cash savings required to start even the smallest
shop. Also few were interested in entering trade. Those who
obtained any education on the whole preferred white-collar
jobs. Africans have in fact been late-comers to trading in Tanganyika, but in the last twenty years or so they have made considerable progress.

There are three prime reasons why they have not progressed
beyond their present stage in the wholesale and retail trade.
One is the general lack of commercial experience and basic
knowledge of trading techniques. The second is the absence
of a competitive business outlook. The third is the absence of
a natural ladder of progress for the African trader to climb,
from his start as a small trader to his establishment as a
successful wholesaler; or, more precisely, a ladder does exist
but it has several missing rungs.

Very few Africans who open a small shop have had any pre-

vious experience of carrying on any form of commercial activity. Many cannot read or write. Many do not understand the
basic concepts of profit and loss. Money put into the till from
daily sales is often thought of as "profit". It is often not realised that fresh stock will have to be bought with this cash in
order to carry on the business. Many shops are opened more
as a status symbol, or possibly to act as a local social centre,
rather than as a commercial enterprise. A great many shops
are only a part-time business, a side-line of another activity,
usually farming. In rural areas there may be no great harm
in this, if the shop is open for only part of the day, as long as
the opening hours are generally known and adhered to. But
this is seldom the case. The shop is opened at irregular
times, and often a wife or child is left in charge, who knows
even less than the owner about running the business.

The background of most Africans born in rural areas does
not include any idea of a competitive business outlook. This
is a concept quite foreign to the traditional social system
among Africans. Not only is active competition with one's
neighbours frowned on, but if one's business prospers, one is
expected to support an ever-widening circle of relations. It
thus becomes impossible to plough back profits and build an
expanding business. Very few successful African traders
operate their businesses in their home areas. It is usually
necessary for them to move right away, to another region,
if possible.

In most parts of the world successful shopkeepers gain
their commercial experience by working to begin with in
someone else's business. Very few Africans have been able
to do this. Almost all the wholesalers and retailers who
employ paid staff are Asian or Arab. The Africans employed
in the small number of European firms are usually of comparatively high educational qualifications and would aspire to
being something more than a small retailer. Scarcely any
Asian or Arab businesses employ any Africans, except to do
manual labour. The one major exception to this is those
produce dealers and wholesalers who run branch shops with
an African manager in charge of each branch. These men
often gain valuable commercial experience, but they have
always been few in number.

For several very good reasons Asian firms have not employed, and still do not employ, African sales or clerical
staff. The most important is that almost all Asian businesses
are family businesses. There are almost always plenty of
members of the family to undertake all the sales and clerical

work. If an outsider is employed this normally deprives a
member of the family of a job. As the system of bargaining
is almost universal, it is usually necessary to have a member
of the family or an experienced man as a salesman. An inexperienced African salesman would be unlikely to fulfil this
function satisfactorily. It is also feared that an outsider
would give away business secrets, while it would be useless
in most businesses to employ an African on the accounts side,
as few accounts are kept in English or Swahili. Finally, it
must be pointed out that until recently there were few Africans
with the necessary educational qualifications who wanted to go
into trade.

Since, for all these reasons, Asians have not employed
Africans in responsible positions in their businesses, this
method of gaining commercial knowledge and experience has
not normally been open to Africans. This brings us round to
the problem of the inadequacy of the ladder of progress for
the African trader.

The usual life story of a successful Asian businessman
begins with his working as an assistant in someone else's,
usually a relation's, business. When he has saved enough,
he sets up on his own, usually in a rural area, and often with
part of his stock on credit from some relative. If his business prospers and he is able to plough back some of his profits, he eventually moves to a larger trading centre or town
and starts doing business as a sub-wholesaler, building this
up in turn into a full-scale wholesale business. It is usually
a long and arduous process, and few who start at the bottom
manage to rise beyond the sub-wholesaling level at the most.

However, the African trader usually has to start without
any previous commercial experience and without any goods
on credit from a relation. He normally starts with a small
shop selling only local 'convenience' goods, such as sugar,
salt, kerosene etc. As has already been pointed out (see
page 98), it is usually very difficult for a small retailer
of this sort to expand his business sufficiently and build up a
large enough stock to attract customers from further afield,
who then make their special purchases from him, i.e., of
clothing, utensils etc., rather than merely buying their day-
to-day requirements.

The next stage, of changing from a successful medium-
sized retailer to being a sub-wholesaler in a trading centre,
is even more difficult to achieve. It normally means invest-
ing a comparatively large sum in new buildings in the trading
centre, as well as in enlarged stock. However, the main

difficulty is that of having to compete directly for the first time on their home ground, as it were, with anything between perhaps five and twenty Asian traders, who have had many years experience of the sub-wholesaling business, while the African trader moving in has probably had very little.

Sub-wholesaling at this level is usually extremely competitive. Furthermore, there is undoubtedly a tendency for established traders anywhere, of whatever race, to try to prevent the establishment of a new, directly competitive business, which, if successful, will inevitably reduce their share of the local trade.

What steps can be taken to assist African traders? There is no doubt that priority should be given to increased commercial education and instruction. There are thousands of small shopkeepers who are just managing to make a living out of their shops, but will never make a real success of them, unless they are shown the elementary techniques of running a shop efficiently. Not only do these shopkeepers have practically no idea of how to run a small shop, they are also, because of their ignorance, liable to be the victims of all sorts of sharp practices. They can easily be confused over weights and quantities and very often prices also. They are often ignorant of the quality of much of the goods they are buying. It is a very general practice for wholesalers and sub-wholesalers to unload dead stock on these small traders, if this is at all possible. However, the problem of giving information and advice to all these small traders is very great, as they are widely scattered, often in the remotest areas. Few can leave their homes and shops for any length of time to attend a course of instruction, and in any case it is doubtful whether any form of academic instruction, however simple, would be really effective. Practical instruction and demonstration in the retailer's own shop seem to be the best answer. This means in effect a commercial extension service comparable to the agricultural extension service.

For the larger African retailers the most important requirement again seems to be advice and instruction, though the most frequently heard request is for loans. This is equally true of the small retailers. The request for a loan has become something of a standard procedure among African traders. However, though African retailers may lack capital, the more serious drawback is their lack of knowledge and experience in the use of such capital as they do have. There is probably not one in a hundred of the small retailers, who, if given a loan, would know how to use it effectively to expand

his business. For most small traders a loan is merely a
welcome windfall. The first requisite is more knowledge and
experience. When this has been acquired, then the most promising traders can be helped with loans, but it would be
possible to make loans totalling hundred of thousands of dol -
lars to small traders, and to have absolutely nothing to show
for it, unless the scheme were supervised with great care.
Loans, together with advice and information, to very carefully
selected applicants, to enable them to expand from a small
local shop to a more general store by increasing their stock
and perhaps improving their premises, could however achieve
a very useful purpose.

For the large African retailers lack of capital can also
prove a problem but again lack of knowledge is usually more
serious. A successful go-ahead retailer with a turnover of
$4, 200 or more a year, of which there are a good many, can
usually obtain a certain amount of credit from his suppliers,
and if he has kept a bank account for a few years, especially
if he owns the title to any property, he can often obtain a
loan from his bank. This is not always the case, as some
bank managers take much more trouble than others to go into
the applications of African traders for loans. Investigations
of this sort can be very time-consuming, especially in relation to the size of the sums of money involved, but this must
be an expanding field for banking in the future, and though a
disproportionate amount of trouble may be needed to develop
it at this stage, this trouble must be considered an investment for the future.

Another measure which could greatly assist small traders
is the setting up of wholesale co-operative societies in the
towns and trading centres, of which these traders could become members, and from which they could obtain both good
service and fair prices. The problems connected with setting
up these wholesale co-operative societies are considered in
more detail below. Other measures designed to help African
traders, for instance those connected with weights and measures, have been discussed above.

THE DEVELOPMENT OF CONSUMER CO-OPERATIVES

Up to 1961 the co-operative movement in Tanganyika concentrated on the setting up of marketing co-operatives. Very
few consumer co-operatives had been registered. However,

that year, the government decided to take vigorous steps
to encourage the setting up of wholesale and retail co-operative societies, and the important first step of inaugurating
the Co-Operative Supply Association of Tanganyika Ltd.,
(COSATA) was taken, with Amiran Ltd., from Israel, as
managing agents. The objects of COSATA are to encourage
the growth of a consumers' co-operative movement by
setting up branches and by the formation of affiliated societies for the supply of goods of all kinds to their members in
wholesale and retail quantities.

Retail co-operative societies were opened in the main
towns, Dar es Salaam to begin with. The purpose of these
societies is, of course, to help the consumer by supplying
him with goods at competitive prices and by enabling him to
share in the trading profits of the society by becoming a
member. The retail co-operatives are for the benefit of the
consumers. As far as the small African traders are concerned, they merely provide additional competition. It is
true that there are few African traders in the large towns, and
the retail co-operatives may provide the best way to enable
Africans to obtain a share of the urban retail trade. On the
other hand, the setting up of these societies will make it more
difficult for independent African retailers to operate successfully in the towns, and it may tend to perpetuate the exceedingly
unsatisfactory present position, whereby African retailers are
all located in the rural areas and seldom challenge the Asian
and Arab retailers in the towns and trading centres.

Individual African traders will never make any real progress in the wholesale trade until they are able to carry on
successful retail businesses in the towns in direct competition with Asian and Arab traders, and it seems necessary to
give them every assistance to do this. Fortunately the setting up of wholesale co-operative societies should help to do
just this.

There is a very widespread desire among African retailers
to form wholesale co-operative societies in the towns and
trading centres. These societies will supply the retailers'
requirements in wholesale quantities at fair prices. The traders themselves will form the membership and will, of course,
share in the profits.

Clearly wholesale co-operative societies of this type can
have a very important role to play in trade in Tanganyika. If
efficiently managed, they can greatly assist African traders
by providing goods at fixed and competitive prices accompa-

nied by fair and honest dealing. They can do a very great
deal towards raising the general standard of wholesaling by
setting examples all over the country of a modern, efficiently
run wholesale business, using up-to-date techniques and trading methods. If these wholesale co-operatives are well run,
providing good service, good layout and display, fair weights
and prices, and perhaps advice to their members, they could
do more than any other single factor to help the African
traders.

If COSATA is able to set up a chain of wholesale societies
across the country, it will be in a very strong position to
supply goods at very competitive prices. Throughout the
world, at a certain stage in the development of a country's
distribution system, the establishment of chain stores is
found to be a very successful and profitable development.
It seems surprising at first sight that no real chain stores
have been established in Tanganyika to date. A few of the
large importing houses have three or four branches, but these
hardly constitute a chain, and have not been expanded signifi-
cantly in the last twenty years. Some of the produce and
piecegoods traders have perhaps one or two wholesale
branches, but never enough to constitute a chain.

The advantages of a chain wholesale organisation would be
considerable. Even firms with only one or two branches are
almost always in a very strong position compared with individual traders. An efficient chain organisation is able to
make considerable savings by means of a centralised buying
and importing policy; it can make much better use of available capital and stocks; it is in a strong position to obtain
local foodstuffs at advantageous prices all over the country.
COSATA should be in a position to take advantage of all these
favourable factors.

If there are all these advantages, why have chain wholesalers not been established already in Tanganyika? The
European importing houses did in fact establish chains in the
inter-war years. The four or five branches that some of
them had were all that the volume of trade in those days
would justify. The reason why these chains have not expanded
at all in the last twenty years is that the importing houses have
been fighting a rearguard action against the encroachment into
what used to be their sector of the business by local, mainly
Asian, firms in the bazaar trade. The lines which they handle
have been reduced in number, and they have not felt able to
expand their selling organisations.

Why then have none of the Asian firms established more

extensive chains? The answer may partly have been that the
establishment of a chain requires large sums of capital,
which Asian businessmen preferred to invest in other ways.
Probably the more important reason was lack of available
management skill. Almost all Asian firms are family
businesses. Each wholesale establishment of any size needs
at least two experienced members of the family to run it. Very
few families can muster more than, say, six members who
have had enough experience and can be relied on to run a full-
scale branch, hence the number of branches is normally limited to about three. Paid management is usually not found to
be satisfactory. A lack of trust, perhaps rightly, exists.
Any manager who is efficient and ambitious prefers to set up
on his own, where he has a chance of big capital gains,
rather than merely earning a usually meagre salary plus what
he can pick up on the side. The problem of finding efficient
and trustworthy management is a very serious one, and has
been an important factor in restricting the expansion of many
Asian businesses.

Clearly COSATA is faced with an excellent opportunity at
the present time to set up a highly successful chain wholesaling organisation. However a number of problems have
also to be faced. The main one, of course, is again management.

There is a widespread belief among African traders that
there is little more to the setting-up and successful running
of a wholesale co-operative than collecting members, regis-
tering the society and appointing a committee. It seems to be
generally forgotten that a wholesale co-operative store will
still have to compete with a great many long-established traders. We have already seen that the wholesaling of bulk lines
to African traders is the most competitive and cut-throat sector of the whole distribution system. A successful wholesale
co-operative has to be run efficiently, and this means that an
experienced and honest manager must be employed.

Unfortunately, as we have seen, there are, practically
speaking, no Africans with experience of managing a wholesale business. Non-African managers will have to be found,
who can manage the co-operative and at the same time train
a cadre of African managers for the future. Unfortunately,
these managers are unlikely to be acquainted with local conditions, sources of supply, consumer preferences and so on,
so that initially, at any rate, they will be at a disadvantage
compared with the established wholesalers.

Besides management problems, there are other problems

also facing the new wholesale co-operatives. We have seen
that most Asian wholesalers are family concerns and that
this helps to keep overheads down to a very low level. Co-
operatives will have to employ salaried staff, who will work
fixed hours. More elaborate books and stock records will
need to be kept than those kept by the average Asian firm.
All this will greatly increase the level of the overheads. Co-
operatives also will presumably not be able to supply goods
on credit to retailers, and this will gravely restrict their
ability to compete with independent wholesalers, at least as
far as supplying the larger African retailers is concerned.

COSATA and the wholesale co-operatives start with the
great advantage of forming a country-wide chain, with all the
savings in costs which this is likely to produce. But against
this must be set the problems and disadvantages listed above.
It is greatly to be hoped, however, that it will be possible to
overcome these problems and that COSATA will be able to
establish a successful organisation which will raise the
standard of wholesaling in Tanganyika and greatly assist the
small African trader.

GLOSSARY

Americani - grey, unbleached cotton cloth.

Atta - coarse wheat flour.

Dagaa - small, dried fish caught in the East
      African lakes.

Dhal - lentils, used mainly in vegetable curries
      and soups.

Duka - shop, normally used to describe a small
      African-owned shop.

Ghee - clarified butter.

Kaniki - black cotton cloth, worn wrapped round
      the body.

Khanga - printed cotton squares worn by women,
      normally bought in pairs, one to be
      wrapped round the body, the other over
      the head in the manner of a shawl.

Khanzu - a robe stretching from the neck to the
      feet.

Kikoi - white loin cloth with a coloured border.

Kitenge - plain loin cloth.

Pombe - local beer, normally brewed from maize.

Shamba - agricultural holding or small farm.

Shuka - a form of robe.

APPENDIX: TRADING LICENCES BY DISTRICTS, 1960-61

	DAR ES SALAAM	EASTERN REGION							
		Baga-moyo	Kilosa	Kisarawe	Mafia	Moro-goro	Rufiji	Ulanga	Total
Wholesaler (Import (i) and Export	231	-	1	-	-	2	-	2	5
(ii)	28	-	-	-	-	4	-	-	4
Wholesaler (Import (i) only)	507	-	2	-	-	5	-	-	7
(ii)	15	-	-	-	-	6	-	-	6
Wholesaler only (i)	356	17	48	13	12	53	26	21	190
(ii)	16	-	7	-	-	14	4	22	47
Commission agents	48	-	-	-	-	-	-	-	-
Broker	52	-	-	-	-	-	-	-	-
Total Wholesalers	1,253	17	58	13	12	84	30	45	259
Non-African Retail- (i) er(incl.import)	82	-	-	-	-	2	-	-	2
(ii)	7	-	-	-	-	-	-	-	-
Non-African Produce buyer (incl.retailer)	48	28	211	107	38	154	51	13	602
Non-African Retailer	1,338	83	110	46	10	224	20	24	517
Total Non-African Retailers	1,475	111	321	153	48	380	71	37	1,121
Total Wholesalers and Non-African Retailers	2,728	128	379	166	60	464	101	82	1,380
African Retailers	230	350	666	616	282	1,169	600	474	4,157
Total Traders (excl. itinerant)	2,958	478	1,045	782	342	1,633	701	556	5,537
Itinerant Traders	53	80	155	73	5	327	110	13	763

APPENDIX: (Continued)

LAKE REGION

	Geita	Kwimba	Maswa	Mwanza	Musoma	North Mara	Shin-yanga	Ukerewe	Total
Wholesaler (Import (i) and Export)	-	-	1	23	-	-	-	-	24
(ii)	-	-	2	20	-	-	-	-	24
Wholesaler (Import (i) only)	-	10	12	104	27	13	22	18	206
(ii)	-	2	4	15	4	3	14	2	34
Wholesaler only (i)	25	42	54	80	3	6	4	17	241
(ii)	-	3	-	7	-	-	4	3	17
Commission agents	-	-	-	2	-	-	-	-	2
Broker	-	-	-	1	-	-	-	-	1
Total Wholesalers	25	57	73	252	34	22	46	40	549
Non-African Retail- (i) er (incl. import)	2	1	-	23	35	9	10	-	80
(ii)	-	-	-	1	1	-	-	-	2
Non-African Produce buyer (incl. retailer)	150	74	102	84	53	35	135	14	647
Non-African Retailer	48	35	86	333	65	13	266	68	914
Total Non-African Retailers	200	110	188	441	154	57	411	82	1,643
Total Wholesalers and Non-African Retailers	225	167	261	693	188	79	457	122	2,192
African Retailers	1,450	864	1,303	1,759	880	663	485	416	7,820
Total Traders (excl. itinerant)	1,675	1,031	1,564	2,452	1,068	742	942	538	10,012
Itinerant Traders	85	124	251	142	298	141	280	89	1,410

APPENDIX: (Continued)

WESTERN REGION

	Kahama	Kasulu	Kibondo	Kigoma	Mpanda	Nzega	Tabora	Ufipa	Total
Wholesaler (Import (i) and Export	-	-	1	10	3	-	9	9	32
(ii)	-	-	-	6	-	1	4	-	11
Wholesaler (Import (i) only)	4	-	2	17	1	6	46	4	80
(ii)	-	-	-	1	-	1	4	-	6
Wholesaler only (i)	39	5	11	17	14	26	50	19	181
(ii)	-	5	-	5	-	-	9	-	19
Commission agents	-	-	-	-	-	-	-	-	-
Broker	-	-	-	-	-	-	-	-	-
Total Wholesalers	43	10	14	56	18	34	122	32	329
Non-African Retail- (i)	-	-	-	-	-	2	-	-	2
er (incl. import) (ii)	-	-	-	-	-	-	-	-	-
Non-African Produce buyer (incl. retailer)	66	19	23	46	86	181	151	64	636
Non-African Retailer	35	8	6	74	-	98	215	4	440
Total Non-African Retailers	101	27	29	120	86	281	366	68	1,078
Total Wholesalers and Non-African Retailers	144	37	43	176	104	315	488	100	1,407
African Retailers	398	287	348	374	331	813	753	1,018	4,322
Total Traders (excl. itinerant)	542	324	391	550	435	1,128	1,241	1,118	5,729
Itinerant Traders	142	107	231	31	68	305	163	66	1,113

APPENDIX: (Continued)

		Kilwa	Lindi	Masasi	Mtwara	Naching-wea	Newala	Songea	Tunduru	Total
						SOUTHERN REGION				
Wholesaler (Import and Export	(i)	-	17	-	5	1	3	-	-	26
	(ii)	1	9	-	14	-	1	3	-	28
Wholesaler (Import only)	(i)	-	32	-	9	1	1	-	1	43
	(ii)	1	7	-	4	-	-	-	1	13
Wholesaler only	(i)	8	38	36	29	13	14	21	6	165
	(ii)	5	25	27	13	2	4	31	17	124
Commission agents		-	-	-	-	-	-	-	-	-
Broker		-	-	-	-	-	-	-	-	-
Total Wholesalers		15	128	63	74	17	23	55	25	399
Non-African Retailer -	(i)	1	2	1	1	-	-	-	-	5
er (incl. import)	(ii)	4	1	-	-	1	-	-	-	6
Non-African Produce buyer (incl. retailer)		23	84	64	32	24	86	14	31	358
Non-African Retailer		34	116	6	8	17	32	49	16	278
Total Non-African Retailers		62	203	71	41	42	118	63	47	647
Total Wholesalers and Non-African Retailers		77	331	134	115	59	141	118	72	1,041
African Retailers		330	623	491	347	84	318	911	102	3,206
Total Traders (excl. itinerant)		407	954	625	462	143	459	1,029	174	4,247
Itinerant Traders		67	101	5	223	13	47	28	13	497

APPENDIX: (Continued)

	SOUTHERN HIGHLANDS REGION					
	Chunya	Iringa	Mbeya	Njombe	Rungwe	Total
Wholesaler (Import and Export) (i)	1	3	5	-	1	10
(ii)	-	-	-	-	1	1
Wholesaler (Import only) (i)	-	22	28	2	27	79
(ii)	-	-	-	-	3	3
Wholesaler only (i)	3	31	79	21	43	177
(ii)	-	-	-	5	7	12
Commission agents	-	2	2	-	-	4
Broker	-	-	-	-	-	-
Total Wholesalers	4	58	114	28	82	286
Non-African Retail - (i) er (incl. import)	-	9	6	-	2	17
(ii)	-	-	-	-	1	1
Non-African Produce buyer (incl. retailer)	18	119	75	20	40	272
Non-African Retailer	9	162	92	24	38	325
Total Non-African Retailers	27	226	173	44	81	615
Total Wholesalers and Non-African Retailers	31	348	287	72	163	901
African Retailers	209	815	911	1,026	710	3,671
Total Traders (excl. itinerant	240	1,163	1,198	1,098	873	4,572
Itinerant Traders	120	98	244	270	51	783

APPENDIX: (Continued)

TANGA REGION

	Handeni	Lushoto	Pangani	Pare	Tanga	Total
Wholesaler (Import and Export) (i)	-	1	3	-	15	19
(ii)	-	2	-	-	31	33
Wholesaler (Import only) (i)	-	15	2	2	102	121
(ii)	-	3	-	-	29	32
Wholesaler only (i)	6	29	10	3	38	86
(ii)	4	5	-	-	3	12
Commission agents	-	-	-	-	2	2
Broker	-	-	-	-	1	1
Total Wholesalers	10	55	15	5	231	306
Non-African Retail- (i) er (incl. import)	-	8	-	-	34	42
(ii)	-	-	-	-	2	2
Non-African Produce buyer (incl. retailer)	27	52	6	21	71	177
Non-African Retailer	18	243	54	18	811	1,144
Total Non-African Retailers	45	303	60	39	918	1,365
Total Wholesalers and Non-African Retailers	55	358	75	44	1,136	1,671
African Retailers	301	1,119	188	799	1,486	3,893
Total Traders (excl. itinerant)	356	1,477	263	843	2,622	5,564
Itinerant Traders	357	1,463	82	210	1,000	3,112

APPENDIX: (Continued)

	WEST LAKE REGION					NORTHERN REGION				
	Bukoba	Karag-we	Bihara-mulo	Ngara	Total	Arusha	Masai	Mbulu	Moshi	Total
Wholesaler (Import and Export) (i)	9	-	1	-	10	17	-	-	17	34
(ii)	4	-	-	-	4	5	-	-	-	5
Wholesaler (Import only) (i)	32	-	-	-	32	51	3	1	90	145
(ii)	6	-	-	-	6	13	-	-	-	13
Wholesaler only (i)	19	7	3	3	32	14	-	6	23	43
(ii)	2	-	-	1	3	6	-	-	-	6
Commission agents	-	-	-	-	-	1	-	-	2	3
Broker	-	-	-	-	-	-	-	-	-	-
Total Wholesalers	72	7	4	4	87	107	3	7	132	249
Non-African Retail- (i) er (incl. import) (ii)	20	-	-	-	20	38	-	7	69	114
	1	-	-	-	1	17	-	3	-	20
Non-African Produce buyer (incl. retailer)	49	-	10	57	116	61	43	102	37	243
Non-African Retailer	149	4	8	36	197	162	59	60	142	423
Total Non-African Retailers	219	4	18	93	334	278	102	172	231	800
Total Wholesalers and Non-African Retailers	291	11	22	97	421	385	105	179	373	1,049
African Retailers	2,201	110	145	342	2,798	595	118	326	1,357	2,396
Total Traders (excl. itinerant)	2,492	121	165	439	3,219	980	223	505	1,730	3,445
Itinerant Traders	1,042	273	202	138	1,655	411	191	281	728	1,611

APPENDIX: (Continued)

	CENTRAL REGION							TOTAL TANGANYIKA
	Dodoma	Kondoa	Manyoni	Mpwapwa	Singida	Iramba	Total	
Wholesaler (Import and Export) (i)	4	-	-	-	1	-	5	396
(ii)	4	-	-	-	-	-	4	142
Wholesaler (Import only) (i)	27	1	-	1	15	-	44	1,264
(ii)	2	-	-	-	-	-	2	130
Wholesaler only (i)	30	9	14	12	18	1	84	1,555
(ii)	5	-	-	-	3	-	8	264
Commission agents	-	-	-	-	-	-	-	59
Broker	-	-	-	-	-	-	-	54
Total Wholesalers	72	10	14	13	37	1	147	3,904
Non-African Retailer (i) (incl. import)	4	-	-	-	8	-	12	376
(ii)	-	-	-	-	1	-	1	40
Non-African Produce buyer (incl. retailer)	86	99	86	97	52	150	570	3,669
Non-African Retailer	163	55	18	44	52	47	429	6,005
Total Non-African Retailers	253	154	104	141	113	247	1,012	10,090
Total Wholesalers and Non-African Retailers	325	164	118	154	150	248	1,159	13,954
African Retailers	692	439	123	165	269	400	2,088	34,581
Total Traders (excl. itinerant)	1,017	603	241	319	419	648	3,247	48,535
Itinerant Traders	170	173	52	31	124	29	579	11,576

General Notes: (i) Principal place of business.
                 (ii) Subsidiary place of business.
The licensing year runs from 1st April, 1960 to 31st March, 1961.

The figures for the District of Nachingwea in the Southern Region and for the sub-district of Mbozi are not available, so that the returns for the previous licensing period have been used. Likewise the return for the Districts of Tunduru, Southern Region, Mbulu, Northern Region and Kahama, Western Region are incomplete, so that again the returns for the previous licensing period have been used. This should affect the figures very little, as changes are only slight from year to year. There was, however, a sharp drop in African trading licences in the Moshi district, Northern Region, and Rungwe District, Southern Highlands Region, in each case to about half the pre- vious year's figures. No explanation for this is available.

Source   Tanganyika Ministry of Finance.